# The 21st Century Revolution

## A Call to Greatness

*Bruce Nixon*

**Bruce Nixon**

Copyright © Bruce Nixon, 2015

Published by Acorn Independent Press Ltd, 2015.

The right of Bruce Nixon to be identified as the Author of the Work has been asserted by him in accordance with the Copyright, Designs and Patents Act 1988.

All rights reserved.

This book is sold subject to the condition it shall not, by way of trade or otherwise, be circulated in any form or by any means, electronic or otherwise without the publisher's prior consent.

Cover photograph reproduced by kind permission of Global Justice Now

ISBN 978-1-911079-03-3

Acorn Independent Press

# *Thanks*

I thank my wife, Suzanne, for supporting and putting up with me whilst I have been writing this book. My friends, John Bell, Val Tomlin and Paul de Hoest, kindly read the first draft of this book and gave me invaluable comments. Over the years, James Robertson has made many contributions to my thinking about global issues and, specifically, on money and taxation. I am grateful to Satish Kumar for his holistic inspiration. Nicklaus Thomas-Symonds gave me insights on statesmanship and how it may emerge. Polly Higgins, Professor Ian Roberts, John Mills of CIVITAS, and friends in the New Economics Foundation, Global Justice Now, Garden Organic, the Soil Association, GM Freeze, Positive Money, Unlock Democracy, the Electoral Reform Society, and the Campaign for Better Transport, have contributed to my understanding of the whole interconnected system and provided solutions.

# *Endorsements*

"This is a book jam-packed with solutions – hurrah! And, it all starts with the self; great change calls on each of us to step up and respond to the call of greatness. Whether it be changing our politics, our monetary system, our laws, our business ethics – at the heart of each resides something truly great. Bruce Nixon brings to life not only what is possible, what is already emerging, and also what could yet come into being."

**Polly Higgins, Barrister, International Ecocide law advocate.**


"This is an amazing book not just because it tells us what's wrong with our society and how to put it right – but because it is full of hope and love for people and our planet. The world is a better place for The 21st Century Revolution – A Call to Greatness, and its author, Bruce Nixon the book inspires me to help make the 21st century revolution happen."

**Neal Lawson, Chair of Compass**


"A fascinating read and a really good contribution to the debate about the future of democracy."

**Katie Ghose, Chief Executive of the Electoral Reform Society.**

"The greatest problem of our age is disempowerment – part of a political project to shift ordinary people out of power and out of politics, to leave them content to judge their identity by the brand of smart phone they rent. Bruce Nixon lays out the fullest dimension of this disempowerment and its fatal consequences. But he also outlines a way out, a way for all of us to become real citizens in a real democracy. The call to greatness not only refers to our own personal liberation from the shackles of disempowerment, but to the scale of the collective endeavour it will allow us to embark on saving our species. It doesn't get much bigger."

**Nick Dearden, Director, Global Justice Now**

"Read this excellent analysis of what's gone wrong, take heart, and fight for positive change!"

**Yvonne Roberts, Journalist and Fellow of the Young Foundation**

"Don't despair – read this book! We can have a new economic system that works for people and planet, if enough of us meet the current (huge) challenges head-on and summon the greatness that each of us are capable of. Bruce Nixon brilliantly sets out a course of action and hope."

**Stewart Wallis, Executive Director, New Economics Foundation**

*"We need to be both planning for a better world and actively setting out a route towards it. That needs the input of the many and the democratic focus of this book is very much welcome, as is its understanding that our economic, social and environmental crises and the solutions to them are interlinked."*

**Natalie Bennett, Leader, Green Party of England and Wales**


*"Bruce highlights the harmful consequences of our debt-based money system and the need to change the way money is created."*

**Ben Dyson, Founder of Positive Money**


*"Bruce's book is a comprehensive account of the social and political obstacles standing between us and a more sustainable future. In response to that, he proposes a collective approach, and that's absolutely right – if we want change, people power is going to be at the heart of it."*

**Dale Vince, Ecotricity Founder**

# *Other Books and Writings by Bruce Nixon*

*A Better World is Possible – What needs to be done and how we can make it happen*

*Living System – Making sense of sustainability*

*Global Forces – A Guide for Enlightened Leaders*

*Making a Difference – Strategies and Tools for Transforming your Organisation*

*New Approaches to Management Development*

*Articles, talks and conference papers: www.brucenixon.com/newwritings.html*

# Contents

Introduction .................................................................. 11

## Part One – Challenges and opportunities – the current system is a rip-off ........................... 23

1. I listen to a lot of people in all walks of life ............... 25
2. The multiple challenges we face ................................ 62
3. The environmental challenge
   – we're sleepwalking to disaster ............................... 111
4. A fatally flawed mind-set ........................................ 139
5. Neoliberalism exposed ............................................ 158

## Part Two – Bringing about the revolution – it's already happening; we just need to give it a very strong push ........................................... 179

6. Environmental solutions – before it's too late ........... 181
7. An economy that works for all ................................ 205
8. Resolving conflict without violence
   – Learning to rejoice in difference;
   ending violent conflict and war ............................... 229
9. Transforming democracy – a great
   power shift from politicians to people ..................... 243
10. Conclusion – daring to be great ............................. 272

Resources ................................................................... 277
Appendix on systems thinking ..................................... 296

# Introduction

*"It's OK for you. We and our children will have to face your generation's irresponsibility way beyond 2050."*
**A sixth-former**

As a parent, grandparent and fellow world citizen, that is my starting point.

**We face the greatest challenges in human history.** This book is for people all over the world who want to create a happier, fairer, more peaceful world and prevent environmental catastrophe. It is for people who want to be well-informed. The book will help readers make sense of the situation, find solutions, and decide how they want to participate in bringing about the radical changes that are needed. There is a widespread collapse of confidence in current politics and economics. The challenges are enormous, but so are the opportunities. Change is in the wind all over the world. Change springs out of vision and hope. This book will provide both. When great shifts come, they tend to come fast; the old order collapses quickly. Remember the fall of the Berlin Wall.

There is widespread anti-establishment sentiment. The economic policies of the past 35 years are being challenged, especially by younger people; so is the way we have done politics for the past 70 years. Yet radical new policies, large-scale events, and campaigns involving thousands often go unreported in the mainstream media. There is so much positive news the conventional media doesn't give us. That will be remedied in this book.

It is now 23 years since the Kyoto Protocol was adopted in Kyoto, Japan on 11th December 1997. Yet decisive action has not been agreed or taken. The 21st annual session of the International Climate Change Conference is to be held in Paris from the 30th November to 11th December 2015. There must be a breakthrough. Sir David King, UK's Special Representative for Climate Change, whilst hopeful of this session, says climate change is the *"biggest threat facing mankind at this moment"* and reaching agreement is *"more critical to the future of our civilization than 1945"*, when the UN was created following two World Wars.

This year also marks the 800th anniversary of Magna Carta. There are growing calls for radical reform of outdated democratic institutions, and a different way of doing politics. Reform has been obstructed for decades and, in some cases, for over a century. The determination of the suffragist women in the late 19th and early 20th centuries provides a lesson for us. They won the vote. We need to win a lot more.

As George Monbiot says:
*"Society moves from the margins, not the centre."*

I compare our situation today with the dark days before World War Two. Then, Britain faced a Nazi invasion, a complete takeover of Europe, and world domination. Today, the challenge is even greater: the catastrophic effects of climate change and destruction of the ecological system. In 1940, George Orwell wrote:

### the 21st century revolution

*"The initiative will have to come from below. ... I only know that the right men will be there when the people say they really want them, for it is movements that make leaders and not leaders' movements. And ... A real shove from below will accomplish it."* **Why I Write – The English Revolution**

And so it was and the War was won.

Today, we are again confronted with leadership failure. Leadership will be a major theme throughout this book. The challenges are great. Yet ecologically and economically illiterate political leaders are failing to tackle them. The obsession with unsustainable growth, measured by GDP (Gross Domestic Product), on a finite planet we are warming up is madness. It will lead to growing violence, resource wars and migration. Instead of GDP, we need wellbeing as our measure of progress.

**A great, big scam robs us and threatens our survival.** In 2008, the Western world suffered the worst financial crisis since the Wall Street Crash of 1929. Its primary causes were irresponsible banking and too much lending and borrowing. The recession that followed soon led to austerity policies implemented to varying degrees throughout Europe.

Neoliberal ideology (explained in Chapter 5) has dominated economic policy for 35 years. It has profoundly affected our values and how we treat our fellow human beings. Blatant greed at the top is shocking. Corporate responsibility has become an oxymoron. In this environment, it's hard for companies and their leaders to be responsible and survive.

**bruce nixon**

In the UK, the financial crisis gave the Tory-led Coalition a golden opportunity to decimate the public sector. Austerity, based on ideology, not on sound economics, was forced through by an illiterate government without a mandate to do so. Deep cuts will continue under the new administration. These hindered and continue to hinder recovery and deficit reduction. Every day there has been news of the dire consequences of counterproductive cuts. Whilst the rich got richer, and doubled their wealth, average, real incomes fell by 8%, compared with 2007. For those in work, they still have not recovered. Ordinary people who create wealth are robbed in ways I shall explain.

Similar policies have been implemented in Europe with similar results, adversely affecting young people, particularly in Greece and Spain. Fundamentally, they are the same policies imposed on poor and developing countries by Western institutions for decades.

Greece, with its highly dysfunctional economy in urgent need of reform, is the current most disastrous example: a combination of irresponsible lending followed by insistence on debt repayment and austerity led to deep depression and 25% unemployment. Youth unemployment is 60% (50% in Spain). Finally, in the Greek referendum, 61% of voters decisively rejected a further international bailout from the Troika (IMF, EU and European Central Bank) with continuing austerity attached.

Austerity is like draining a patient's blood to purge the evil humours once thought to cause disease. Of course, all the bloodletting did was to make the patient weaker and more likely to succumb. Luckily, most of us are made of stronger stuff. But millions of people are needlessly suffering; it's a shameful waste of human potential.

These policies will continue unless active citizens demand change.

In the UK, we've allowed ourselves to be conned (helped by campaign advisers, some with dubious connections) and ruled by an out of touch political class, in the pockets of the Big Banks, Big Business, and the super-rich, who, because of dwindling party membership, that used to be millions, fund their campaigns.

*"Political language is designed to make lies sound truthful and murder respectable, and to give an appearance of solidity to pure wind."* **George Orwell** in **Why I Write – The English Revolution.**

**We need a very different agenda.** A system based on short-term self-interest rather than generosity of spirit has no future in the 21$^{st}$ century world. The same applies to foreign policy. The recent election campaigning in the UK was based on fear. Instead, we need a vision that uplifts and engages people in a great, new endeavour that creates a prosperous society in which everyone benefits.

As Yvonne Roberts says:
*"A good state would give each of us the chance to thrive. A dynamic, modern country should not treat its citizens as passive clients, but as agents for a greater change... An opportunity for a genuinely participatory, challenging, creative and active citizenship requires something different*

**bruce nixon**

*from the state than the retail politics of selling 'the offer' to the electorate."*

Neal Lawson, Chair of Compass, says:
*"The mission of government should be to unleash the energy and potential of everyone to transform their workplaces, communities and lives."*

**There is a growing awakening throughout the world.** The story of Syriza in Greece has much in common with Spain's Podemos and Scotland's Independence Campaign. Jeremy Corbyn's surprise bid to lead and transform the UK Labour party is attracting rapidly growing support, especially from younger people. It is part of the widespread rejection of the economic policies of the past 35 years and distaste for the behaviour of political leaders. More is to come.

People are realising that capitalism and democracy in their current forms are failing us. There is a growing rebellion against the current order. Younger people, angry about the injustice of their situation, are opting out of conventional politics and exploring new ways of bringing about change, often bottom up, and creating new businesses. Politics as we know it is a sideshow. The mainstream is happening outside party politics and the daily news. There is a huge discourse on the internet that many people are unaware of. All over the world, people are seeking alternatives. You will read about it in this book.

The need for visionary leadership at every level is greater than ever before. Patriarchal, top-down leadership is obsolete. People want enabling leadership that releases

## the 21st century revolution

human creativity and bottom-up change. But major transformation will not take place unless many more people get involved and demand change. Far more pressure is needed.

Depending on the choices we make, collectively and individually, we could be at the beginning of a benign revolution or a breakdown of society leading to extremism. This particularly applies to people who feel excluded. Young women and men travel to Syria; others drop out.

***I listen to a lot of people in all walks of life*** in many countries (Chapter 1). What they told me inspired me to write this book. Many are disheartened, angry about the current situation, and feel powerless. Following the results of the recent UK General Election, they are even angrier and more disheartened. It is outrageous that a first past the post voting system results in an unrepresentative parliament, and a Tory government with less than 37% of the vote, representing 24% of the population, continues to inflict extreme policies upon the nation without a mandate. If they do not take this into account, there will be a lot of strife.

Already numerous demonstrations are taking place; many more are planned.

Until nations have properly representative government, things are unlikely to change significantly for the better.

A lot more of us need to get angry. Anger should never be acted out, but it provides the passion and energy needed for constructive change. The fact is: we need a non-violent revolution – not just in the UK but all over the West. We should be grateful that we can protest, usually without being imprisoned, tortured or shot. Also, we have the rule of law.

*"The future has already arrived. It's just not evenly distributed yet."* **William Gibson**

This future could bring a massive transfer of power away from the grip of government and big business to ordinary people and their local communities, if we choose to make it happen. Being cynical or pessimistic won't help.

**The 21$^{st}$ Century Revolution is already happening.** Every century has its revolutions, political and industrial. The first two industrial revolutions were based on coal, then oil and gas. The third may be based on solar power, hi-tech, bioscience, the World Wide Web, personal and collective empowerment, and the need to respond to ecological disaster.

In his book, *An Optimist's Tour of the Future*, Mark Stevenson gives an exciting account of emerging scientific and technological innovations likely to transform our lives and the world as we know it. Many are benign. Undoubtedly, many of these developments will bring enormous benefits, particularly in the area of human health. They could reduce costs and devolve power. However, I am cautious; they could result in the even greater concentration of power and wealth in the hands of the few, and further alienation of human beings from nature of which we are part. And these developments will not help unless we are determined to resolve economic inequality, entrenched power structures and act on the urgent need to conserve and sustain a living planet. The danger is we'll be deluded by techno-fixes.

***Systems thinking.*** Central to this book is the idea that the immense challenges we face require whole system change, not partial fixes. Everything is interconnected; we are part of one whole; we are part of nature; we are all one. Systems thinking is the process of understanding how systems influence one another within a whole. It is an approach to problem solving in which problems are seen as parts of an overall system. Thus, rather than reacting to specific parts, as political leaders tend to, with the danger creating unintended consequences, we need to look at the whole system and identify the fundamental issues before creating solutions.

So **Part One** is a whole system analysis of the current situation. **Part Two** offers a new, better future, and explores how all of us can make it happen. It includes comprehensive proposals for addressing:
- Climate Chaos and destruction of the eco-system
- Economic injustice
- Resolving conflict without violence
- Radical reform of broken and corrupt, top-down politics
- And, that key part, what you, the reader, will do

All of which form an inter-related system.

Whilst many of these proposals call for international collaboration, some are specific to the UK, yet equally relevant to other nations. Countries learn from each other.

### bruce nixon

***The next few years are likely to be full of surprises.***
In the UK, the voting system has deprived many people of their wishes. Of almost 31 million people who voted in the recent General Election on the 7$^{th}$ May, 19 million voted for losing candidates. That's 63% of voters who backed a candidate that didn't win, making the majority of voters feel unrepresented. Out of 650 winning candidates, 322 (49%) got less than 50% of the vote.

The Westminster Village is discredited. That was the clear message of the Scottish referendum. People will vote if they believe it will make a difference. An unprecedented 97% registered to vote in the referendum and 84.6% voted, including 16 to 17-year-olds, for the first time. It was the highest vote in the UK since the introduction of universal suffrage. This has increased the pressure for reform. 44.7% voted for independence. As I write, elections are to be held in Spain, Poland, Denmark, Finland, Portugal and Estonia. Debt and austerity have played a major part in creating a desperate situation in Greece. The Greek election was a strong vote of no confidence in the current economic doctrine. At the time of writing, the results of negotiations between the Greek Prime Minister, Alexis Tsipras, and the EU are unknown but are likely to be far-reaching.

***We need a great power shift – a peaceful revolution.***
A revolution is swelling at the moment, as evidenced by widespread and growing protests. They will grow. I hope this book will give many people the desire to participate at an epic moment in human history. Currently, power is held by elites who will obstruct anything they think adversely affects their interests. We need a shift of power to people and communities, enabled by a new kind of slimmer state.

## the 21st century revolution

We, seven billion people, need to use our power; otherwise little will change.

This book is a call to ordinary people to be great. Through your relationships with others, you can help create the critical mass required to bring about this great transformation. We can be sure revolution will come from the power and creativity of millions of people. If you are not already involved, I invite you to become part of it. If you are part of it, I hope reading this book will give you even greater power. Being well-informed gives people power; it's essential for an effective democracy. People won't be well-informed if they rely on old media. I endeavour to make sense of the biggest crisis humanity has ever faced. I describe the radical changes that are needed and suggest what you can do to help.

In the Resources section at the end of the book, I offer you many different ways in which you can play your part. There are suggestions at the end of some chapters. References and links are provided conveniently in the text, rather than at the end of the book. Hyperlinks are provided in the e-book version. I have quoted from writings that I believe are particularly useful or articulate, thus introducing you to people you may wish to follow, and sources of further information.

Bruce Nixon October 2015

# *Part One*

## Challenges and opportunities – the current system is a rip-off

This part offers a whole system analysis of the situation we are in. It describes the multiple challenges we face: Climate Chaos, destruction of our habitat, poverty and growing inequality, and how current economic and political systems fail to serve us. It is an exposé of illiterate, Neoliberal economic policies of cuts and austerity, and their disastrous consequences.

The need for systems thinking (Appendix 1 gives a fuller explanation) is central to this book. It is an approach to problem solving in which problems are seen as parts of an overall system. Thus, as said earlier, we need to see the whole system, identify the fundamental issues, and create a coherent strategic vision. The past five years provide many examples of not doing this from which we can learn.

Another recurrent theme is the need for a very different kind of leadership and new ways of doing politics. We

**bruce nixon**

need leaders who see themselves as stewards, leaders who enable the leadership of citizens.

I begin with the views of many people from different walks of life.

# Chapter 1

# *I listen to a lot of people in all walks of life*

Over the past five years, a growing consensus has emerged all over Europe and elsewhere as a result of the imposition of austerity based on Neoliberal ideology and the consequences for ordinary people. Europe's economy is stagnant. People are tired of a negative story and want an alternative, positive narrative that offers a pathway to a flourishing economy in which everyone benefits.

My purpose in this chapter is to explore what we can learn from this experience. Whilst I describe in more detail the situation in the UK, discontent with current politics and economics is widespread and growing all over the world. As George Monbiot says: *"The lights are coming on all over Europe."*

**Listening to people in all walks of life has inspired me to write.** For some reason, people like talking with me. They worry about the environmental crisis, increasing Climate Chaos, growing inequality, and the future of their children and grandchildren. They know something is badly wrong but most feel powerless and don't know what to do. There is a sense that the main political parties offer no real choices and people have no influence. They yearn for visionary, enlightened leadership, an honest leadership they can trust to serve everyone, as opposed to being self-serving. Too much of the discourse in the recent UK General Election was tactical and about instilling fear; people want a unifying vision.

Of course, we need to look to ourselves for inspiration. But we are right to expect much more of political leaders.

**People are angry and frustrated** by the failure of successive governments to act decisively on climate change, ecological destruction, poverty and inequality. Political leaders are part of the problem, not the solution. People doubt the need for harsh austerity and damaging cuts. They witness dire effects on every aspect of society, bearing down on almost everyone, but particularly on poorer people, women, children and younger adults. Young people see fewer opportunities; the chances of buying a home become increasingly remote. Should young people get into debt in order to pay for the nation's higher education, thereby making profits for banks? People realise that their taxes are being used to subsidise employers paying poverty wages and property owners charging too high rents. Taxpayers' money was used to bail out irresponsible bankers whose greed created the financial crisis and who continue to pay themselves far too much; none have gone to prison for what amount to crimes.

For 35 years, successive governments followed Neoliberal policies. Once in power, the Tory-led Coalition scrapped much of the previous government's work, causing distress to dedicated people who worked hard to implement earlier changes. Constant re-organisation is wasteful and destructive. Most often, it is excellent leadership that's required, not another re-structuring. Also, Government does not understand the respective roles of the public and private sectors.

***We continue to lose our local shops.*** Of course, that's partly our responsibility: use them or lose them. Local shops and businesses, often family-run, are at the heart of our communities; they bring more wealth into the local economy than supermarkets and, without them, we have to travel further. As a result, we walk less, drive more, get unhealthier, escalate climate change, and create more pollution, congestion and stress in traffic jams. Unhealthy lifestyles and pollution cost the NHS billions. A local shopkeeper told me: *"Soon there will be no high street local shops."* His rent is rising steadily. He continued: *"Before long, I'll be working just to pay the rent."* Rents are being driven up because property owners can get higher rents from chains. (Local Works proposes a *"Tesco Tax"* on supermarkets, which would provide funds to assist small retail businesses and fund other community purposes. Many local authorities are adopting it. See www.bbc.co.uk/news/business-28495631 www.bbc.co.uk/news/uk-politics-25713946 and www.localworks.org/.)

***People are angered by the little say they have in deciding the future of their communities.*** They regret the loss of really useful local shops, the domination by supermarkets and developers, the steady destruction of historic and beautiful towns, and the little say local people have. Unwelcome developments, without adequate infrastructure or sustainability standards are imposed by developers and a remote borough council. There are insufficient natural resources in the East of England, such as water, to support the rapidly growing developments. Not enough space is made available for growing the local food we shall surely need. Investors, developers, supermarkets and councillors who do not represent the majority of people determine the future of our communities, towns and cities. It should not be like this.

**London's World Heritage Sites are threatened** by super-rich, foreign investors, the sources of whose wealth are highly questionable, wanting a good home for their money, and to make grand, phallic statements. There are plans for more than 230 tower blocks. And what thought is given to the environmental impact of all this construction? London is described as *a "residential tax-haven"*. Of the 12 families and individuals at the top of the Sunday Times Rich List, only two are UK citizens. http://www.thesundaytimes.co.uk/sto/public/richlist/

**Widespread cynicism.** People believe there is little they can do about the environmental crisis or changing things for the better. Polls show increasing cynicism about government and politics. Tony Blair's administration was a period of prosperity and he deserves much credit for improvements in the NHS and education, and reduction in child poverty. But he was a big disappointment. He raised such hopes but turned out to be a Thatcherite with a more acceptable image. Many people felt betrayed when he took the nation into an illegal war against Iraq on the basis of a lie, undermining the UN, and despite nearly two million people demonstrating on the streets of London (a poll put opposition to war at 52% with only 29% in favour). There were global protests – three million on the streets of Rome and anything between 10 and 30 million in cities around the world. Apart from all the deaths, injuries, millions displaced from their homes, and horrors inflicted on civilians and growing chaos in the Middle East, an unrepentant Tony Blair did great damage to the UN and democracy in his country. I frequently hear the failure of these demonstrations used to justify the belief that lobbying and protesting are futile.

*There is nothing we can do.*

**Privatisation.** Whilst the UK Tory-led Coalition steadily privatised public services, the majority of the public are opposed. 68% of the public say the energy companies should be run within the public sector, while only 21% say they should remain in private hands. 66% support re-nationalising the railway companies, while only 23% think they should be run privately – it is argued that could save over £1 billion a year (www.theguardian.com/uk-news/2014/jul/07/labour-stands-firm-rail-renationalisation) and research referred to in this article shows that UK railway subsidies are considerably higher than in other European countries. The British people also strongly prefer a publicly-run National Health Service and Royal Mail, as it was until this year (YouGov: https://yougov.co.uk/news/2013/11/04/nationalise-energy-and-rail-companies-say-public/).

**Underfunding costs more in the long-run.** Key services deprived of the necessary funds and staffing levels put staff under extreme pressure, with service deteriorating as a result. A friend described the appallingly distressing neglect of her elderly mother in hospital at night because not enough nurses were available. David Cameron promised that there would be no top-down reorganisation of the NHS; but there was and it has proved extremely costly – there will be more about this in Chapter 5. King's Fund Chief Executive, Chris Ham, told the BBC:

*"People in the NHS focused on rearranging the deckchairs rather than the core business of improving patient care. That's contributed to the increasing waiting times and declining performance that patients are experiencing."*

He described the reforms as simply *"disastrous"*. Experienced staff left or were made redundant, some with expensive redundancy packages, and were replaced with less experienced staff, costing more again. Some 4,000 have since been rehired. Recently, it emerged that the employment of agency nurses in NHS hospitals had reached £2.6bn a year. That does not include locum doctors at £1,760 per day. Since 2010, 38,419 redundancy packages have cost £1.588bn. Auditors reported concerns about the financial resilience of a third of trusts. Creeping privatisation creates conflicts of interest for medical practitioners. Privatisation has resulted in confidentiality clauses that prevent councillors and the public getting access to key information. These difficulties create huge pressures, adversely affect patient care and staff morale, and create recruitment difficulties. Many newly qualified medics are considering working overseas. Of course, there is much need for improved efficiency and cost savings, but these are difficult to bring about in such circumstances.

There are continuing warnings of a Health Service in crisis and need for vastly increased funding. Sir David Nicholson, retired former Head of NHS England, said £8bn extra funding is needed annually, particularly to remedy staff shortages.

Recently, I listened to a GP who heads up a hospice. Here, I summarise the essence of what she said:

When her father was a GP in the newly-created NHS that inspired the world, it was a calling rather than a job. No more is it a vocation. The 21$^{st}$ century is changing all that for a multitude of reasons. Instead of the patient's interests coming first, commissioning GPs face a conflict of interest. Medical practitioners are distracted by targets and financial objectives. Of course, the books must balance. But that is not the primary goal. Neoliberalism (for a definition see http://www.corpwatch.org/article.php?id=376) has poisoned the nation's values; making money becomes the driving force.

## *Whole system thinking*

This situation is an example of where, instead of constant meddling by politicians, whole system analysis is needed: the fundamental issues are not being tackled. Prevention could make a vast contribution through better health education, changes in lifestyle and diet, heavily taxing sugar and other heath harming products, getting people out of their cars and onto their feet or bicycles, and better help with emotional issues. For example, the Early Intervention Foundation's report, issued shortly before the General Election in 2015, found that:

### bruce nixon

*"... the state spends some £17 billion every year on 'late intervention': picking up the pieces of social problems that affect children and young people, when it would be much better and cheaper to stop them happening in the first place. We have set the target to reduce late intervention spend by 10% – £1.7 billion – between now and 2020, through effective early intervention."*

That is the kind of thinking that should prevail.

A systems approach must involve the whole of the system: the health profession at every level and their patients, and the appropriate think tanks in creating a comprehensive solution.

A friend of mine told me that when he opened his first bank account in 1975 and joined the banking industry in 1985, it was still an industry focussed on service to customers – looking after customers and genuinely helping them with their finances. If that meant directing them down the road to another company that offered better products, they would do so (remember, we did not have *"one-stop shop banks"* then, and the options included mutuals). Nowadays, banking has a *"retailing mentality"* whereby customers are merely fodder for profit making – bank managers are targeted to hit sales levels – they weren't in the past. The bank manager was a respected figure in the local community – no more. Furthermore, UK, unlike Germany, suffers from the lack of smaller competitors to the *"big four"* banks. The good news is an inquiry into the market for current accounts and lending to small and medium-sized businesses has been launched by the Competition and Markets Authority.

## the 21st century revolution

However, the lack of diversity and fundamental change in the UK banking system, combined with high levels of personal debt, render us vulnerable to another major financial collapse.

I listened to the guys at our local household waste and recycling centre, about to be taken over by new owners. They didn't know how their jobs would be affected and they have no pension, apart from the state pension scheme – ours is one of the meanest in Europe (conversation.which.co.uk/money/uk-state-pension-comparison-serps/).

A management consultant friend I used to work with said his clients still want to create good workplaces. But in the present business environment, it becomes harder and harder; leaders are exhausted by the pressure.

A father of two said that education is too important to be in the hands of politicians. Now the chairman of the Headmasters' and Headmistresses' Conference, Dr Martin Stephen, High Master of St Paul's school, recommends that an independent commission is set up to end decades of party political *"tampering"*.

**People feel disenfranchised.** In my home town, a woman friend described our safe seat MP as self-serving; he does not represent many of his constituents' views. She said, "Surely it is his job to represent all his constituents, whether he agrees with them or not." In a recent local by-election, only 24% turned out to vote, and of these 60%, voted for parties other than Conservative. Yet another Conservative was elected. I have been unrepresented for 34 years. Here is a disruptive idea. In Stroud, Richard Wilson said he wanted to win the May 7th Election as a people power MP.

*"From the big votes in Parliament, to what case work should be prioritised. The people of Stroud will always be in charge."*

He says online voting could be utilised by the electorate to tell their MP which way to vote on an issue. This is an exciting model for the future. Every MP should do this.

**There is widespread loss of faith in our institutions.** People see a Government front bench, largely from a privileged class, lacking experience of leadership or ordinary life. Corrupted by big business, their parties and the media supporting them are financed by super-rich donors, their wealth often held in tax-havens. People distrust big businesses and are disgusted with the greed of bankers and top business people, paying themselves excessive salaries and bonuses, rising every year, whilst the real incomes of most people decline.

Trust is at an all-time low. Trust in political leaders, local MPs, Whitehall civil servants, senior EU officials, the BBC, television, journalists, and especially tabloid newspapers, is at a low level. It has dropped markedly since 2003 (YouGov: yougov.co.uk/news/2012/11/13/problem-trust/).

**Alpha males talk of driving change** rather than supporting people in creating it. Michael Gove's education reforms are an example. John Hattie, Professor of Education at the University of Melbourne and Chair of the Australian Institute of Teaching and School Leadership, over 20 years carried out one of the biggest pieces of education research, compiling studies from previous decades and comparing the effect they have on attainment and ability. The results show that the skill of teachers is by far the most important factor, and structural changes have relatively little effect. After a few months, the initial effects of shiny, new buildings, academies and free schools wear off. Teachers and parents know that it is the quality of leadership in a school that counts – whether the school is privatised or not. While I refer to this, should public schools, that only the affluent and foreign very rich can afford, enjoy the advantages of charitable status?

**Whilst talking localism and devolution**, Government micro-managed from the centre. Northern cities like Manchester now demand more powers, as recommended by leading think tank, IPPR (www.ippr.org/about/history). The good news is cross-party support for devolving greater powers to cities, the introduction of Metro Mayors, and substantial investment in radically-improved rail links between Northern cities.

**The financial crisis was used as an excuse for implementing Neoliberal policies.** Austerity defies common sense. It has delayed recovery from the worst recession in more than 100 years. Putting people unnecessarily out of work does immense damage. Austerity damages public services, reduces the tax take needed to reduce public debt and increases personal debt. Above all, it causes distress to millions of people. What is needed is a comprehensive plan to transform the economy. Yet all the parties, except the Scottish National Party and the Green Party, are committed to continuing austerity. So you know what to do: *campaign to change this policy*.

**bruce nixon**

***There was and is no mandate for Austerity.*** When 34.90% of those eligible to vote declined to do so – more about why later – and the Tories won 36.1% and Lib Dems 23%, the Tory-led Coalition had no mandate for austerity. Furthermore, women are not properly represented in Parliament or Government. Women, 52% of Britain's population, made up 22% of MPs and roughly a quarter of the cabinet (following the General Election, this is now 29.4%). Yet women and their children are bearing the brunt of the cuts.

*"In Britain, 70% of the cuts so far have impacted on women; care workers can earn little more than £5 an hour; part-timers, mostly in the private sector, receive 43% less pay than full-time males – all of which is exacerbated by continuing privatisation and the destruction of the public sector that has delivered most for women and their children."*
**Yvonne Roberts**, *The Guardian*, Saturday, 12th July 2014 ([www.theguardian.com/commentisfree/2014/jul/12/feminist-party-women-in-politics](www.theguardian.com/commentisfree/2014/jul/12/feminist-party-women-in-politics))

A very high proportion of UK people of Afro or Afro Caribbean origin, who are also badly affected, are not even registered to vote. We need to worry about that.

***The unemployed and people on low wages are in dire straits.*** There were 1.84 million unemployed in February 2015, of whom nearly a million of under-25s were still unemployed, despite growth. 20% of workers are earning less than a living wage. The 400% growth in the use of food banks and 900,000 people dependent on them for survival in the world's sixth wealthiest country (GDP) is a shocking sign of the times. I listened to many professionals in education, health and other parts of our society who are angered by the destructive effects of ideological policies and senseless cuts.

**Young people are hard hit.** All over Europe, there is a growing rebellion against austerity and Neoliberal policies. Young people are hard hit, particularly in Spain, Greece and Italy. Simply put, these policies are damaging Europe needlessly. Many young people, who should be developing and contributing their skills, thus creating innovation and prosperity, are unable to do so. They face the prospect of significantly lower lifetime income than if they had come of age in a period of full employment. (Thanks to Joseph Stiglitz – *Europe's Austerity Zombies* – www.project-syndicate.org/commentary/joseph-e--stiglitz-wonders-why-eu-leaders-are-nursing-a-dead-theory). For a possible way forward for Greece, see James Robertson's contribution in Chapter 7.

**Mental health is severely underfunded**; pills are prescribed rather than psychotherapy or simple counselling, which in many cases give better results. The failure to provide adequate care for depressed young people has tragic effects. And, though costing more, such help would ultimately save large costs – human, including lost lives, financial, and losses to the economy. The state of the prisons is appalling; the penal system continues to be in need of a radical shift towards far fewer inmates, especially young people, with the emphasis on rehabilitation.

**Cuts in funding the arts**, which the Government did not seem to value, are damaging our cultural life, so important to human health, as well as our economy. Here is another example. Renowned biologist, Jane Goodall, recently denounced a recently inflicted budget cut on Kew Gardens that would result in the loss of 125 jobs.

*"There is a tremendous feeling of anger and frustration there and I share it. This is an unbelievably stupid thing to do. This is the mother of all other botanical research centres. Britain should be proud of it, not dismantling it. It is like tearing up the Union Jack. That is why I wrote my letter. I want my protest to go viral. I want thousands and thousands of people to protest as well."*

Sir David Attenborough, former Kew Gardens Trustee, said the cuts were scandalous.

*"Kew is one of the world's most important botanical institutes and this country depends on it for all kinds of things – for publishing surveys of our plant life, carrying out botanical research, and pinpointing imported plants and other species that customs cannot identify. To treat it like a playground that can be taxed or not, depending on how you feel, is simply an uncivilised, philistine act."* (Source: *Jane Goodall and David Attenborough lead fight to save Kew Gardens*, **Robin McKie**, *The Observer* Science Editor, July 13th, 2014).

How would it be if women were properly represented in Parliament and the Cabinet? My experience is that women often have a very different approach to leadership from which men have much to learn. Fortunately, more and more women are at the forefront of leading fundamental change, as I shall show in Chapter 9: *Transforming Democracy*.

***John Maynard Keynes would be aghast at such follies!*** To make massive cuts in jobs and investment during a recession is lunacy. It turns a recession into a slump. Today, there is even less excuse for it when there is no need to borrow for infrastructure projects, such as upgrading and electrifying railways and building schools and hospitals. Sovereign Money (www.positivemoney.org/our-proposals/sovereign-money-creation/), explained fully in Chapter 6, can provide funding without incurring debt. Cutting budgets, jobs and welfare is a sure way of discouraging business investment. Of course, inefficiency and waste cannot be justified. George Osborne's tax cuts have made little difference to the deficit or National Debt. He made a colossal mistake, like most of his colleagues in Europe. Europe is in stagnation, even Germany. Joseph Stiglitz, writing in September 2014, calculated that, after modest growth, from 1980 onwards, output in the Eurozone today was more than 15% below where it would have been had the financial crisis not occurred; there had been a loss of some $1.6 trillion year, and a cumulative loss of more than $6.5 trillion. The gap is widening, not closing. Normally growth is *faster* than normal as the economy makes up lost ground. (*Europe's Austerity Zombies* by **Joseph Stiglitz**: www.project-syndicate.org/commentary/joseph-e--stiglitz-wonders-why-eu-leaders-are-nursing-a-dead-theory#QJjWxq5L3U0u2Kpe.99

*Failure to understand the difference between personal and public debt.* George Osborne does not appear to understand the important difference between personal and public debt: the former, a danger, the latter, required in a recession. This has obstructed solutions to the many challenges we face, including measures to tackle the environmental crisis, green the economy and achieve energy security, which would have helped bring about economic recovery. Austerity measures and cuts have increased personal debt, whilst rising National Debt is estimated to reach £1.36 trillion (*UK Public Spending* www.ukpublicspending.co.uk/uk_national_debt). In 2013, Britain had the fourth highest per capita household debt in the world. This is far more worrying in view of the consequences, if and when interest rates rise (www.cityam.com/1411501631/debt-map).

## *UK National Debt vs the Deficit*

At this point, it may help to clarify the difference between the National Debt and the deficit. There can be confusion, especially as there are conflicting figures from different sources. The UK National Debt, known as the Public Sector Net Cash Requirement (PSNCR), is the total quantity of money borrowed by the UK Government at any one time through the issue of securities by the British Treasury and other government agencies. The deficit is the difference between receipts and spending.

Prime Minister David Cameron was reprimanded in February 2013 by the UK Statistics Authority for creating confusion between the two. In a political broadcast, he said his administration was *"paying down Britain's debts"*. In fact, his administration has been attempting to reduce the deficit, not the overall debt.

**National Debt.** At the end of the financial year ending 2009, the Public Sector National Debt was £724bn. In April 2010, just before David Cameron took office, it had risen to £960 billion, forecast to be £1.5 trillion five years later. At the year ending February 2015, it was £1.469tn. Thus, the debt had increased by just over 50%. Measuring debt as a proportion of gross domestic product (GDP), it had changed from 62% in April 2010 to 80% in February 2015 – an increase of about a third. Forecasts at the time of writing suggest it will peak in the year ending 2017 and then start to fall. However, anything could happen, depending on unpredictable events affecting the world economy. Due to the Government's significant budget deficit, as I write, National Debt is increasing by approximately £107 billion per year, or around £2 billion each week. It has to be said that the UK National Debt is not remarkable, historically or in comparison with other advanced economies.

**Deficit.** At the year ending 2008/09, the deficit was almost £90bn. As of 2011/12, the total deficit was £121 billion. As a result of its efforts to balance the budget, the Coalition Government forecast that the structural deficit would be eliminated in the financial year 2017/18. However, in of April 2015, the International Monetary Fund (IMF), because of their lower estimate of UK productivity, projected a deficit of £7bn by 2019-20, some £14bn worse than Osborne's forecast. The deficit in April 2015 was about £100bn. (Sourced from official statistics and Wiki – en.wikipedia.org/wiki/United_Kingdom_national_debt#cite_note-15)

In December 2014, George Osborne announced dramatic plans to move Britain from the red into the black by further cutting public spending. According to the Institute for Fiscal Studies, his plans *"to put the country back in the black"* by 2018-19 would involve £12bn of welfare cuts and £13bn of savings from government departments. As a percentage of GDP, public spending would fall to its lowest level since the 1930s. The plans, according to the Office for Budget Responsibility, presume the loss of a further one million public sector jobs by 2020, a renewed public sector pay squeeze, and a further freeze on tax credits. GDP growth would remain below the long-run average of 2.5%, rather than generating a sustained recovery capable of making up the loss of output in the recession.

In his Budget speech on 8th July 2015, George Osborne announced that £47.2bn was to be raised through tax increases, with £34.9bn raised from cuts to welfare. This will be extremely painful for millions of people, especially middle-income families, who will take much of the strain of tax credit reforms. £12bn welfare and social security cuts are being phased in over four years rather than two. A Living Wage will be paid to over-25s, starting at £7.20 from April 2016, rising to £9 an hour by 2020. The current minimum wage, for those aged over 21 is £6.50. Previously, he promised he would be spending less than is raised from taxes by 2018-19. Now that target is postponed to 2019-20. The OBR says the National Debt will be £18bn higher by 2020 than promised in March, with £3.5bn of this extra borrowing resulting from these decisions. Shelter, the housing and homelessness charity, says instead of building the homes we need, the Government are cutting housing benefit for renters. Removing this lifeline will mean thousands more families struggling to make ends meet. As a result of scrapping housing benefit, for some 18-21-year-olds, this could result in many young people facing homelessness. Public sector pay rises will be restricted to 1% for a further four years. This is likely to adversely affect recruitment and retention.

## the 21st century revolution

***The cost of servicing the debt.*** The Public Sector Net Cash Requirements (PSNCR) is the interest that the Government must pay to service the existing National Debt. In 2012, the annual cost of servicing the public debt amounted to around £43bn, or roughly 3% of GDP. This is about the same size as the British defence budget. In 2012, the British population was around 64 million, and the debt therefore amounted to a little over £15,000 for each individual Briton, or around £33,000 per person in employment. Each household in Britain pays an average of around £2,000 per year in taxes to finance the interest.

However, by international standards, Britain enjoys very low borrowing costs, largely because the British Government has never failed to repay its creditors. (Source: official statistics and Wiki – en.wikipedia.org/wiki/United_Kingdom_national_debt#cite_note-15.

It is a sad reflection on the state of British politics that, in the run-up to the 2015 General Election, the two largest parties and the Liberal Democrats were, to varying degrees, focussed on further spending cuts and austerity, rather than offering a vision of a sustainable and just economy that would inspire the nation. That was provided by the three women leaders: Nicola Sturgeon, Scottish National Party (SNP), Leanne Wood, Plaid Cymru – the Party of Wales, and Natalie Bennett, Green Party leader. They also oppose retaining weapons of mass destruction. Only Natalie Bennett prioritised the most important issue of all – action to prevent environmental disaster.

It must be said that any recovery has been *in spite of rather than because of* Chancellor of the Exchequer George

Osborne's policies. Although UK GDP was growing above the 2008 pre-recession peak, household consumption, accounting for two-thirds of UK GDP, and high personal debt, boosted by an inflated housing market, was expected to be the main driver. Business investment, productivity and net exports are insufficient. Too dependent on financial services and concentrated in the South East, it is not a balanced economy. George Osborne failed to see the economic benefits and export potential from greening the country. In particular, he failed to exploit the benefits of retro-fitting millions of leaky homes – reducing wasted energy, reducing bills, keeping people warm and providing thousands of jobs.

*"When the facts change, I change my mind."* **John Maynard Keynes**

## *Recovery?*

***How truthful was this "major milestone" in the recovery?*** George Osborne claimed (25th July 2014) a *"major milestone"* in the recovery. The International Monetary Fund estimated that the UK would grow at a quicker rate (3.2%) than all the other G7 countries in 2014. However, he had no reason to congratulate himself. The "recovery" is in spite of his policies.

---

### *Recovery – really?*

- **Employment.** Unemployment had fallen to 6.5%; over 1.1 million new jobs had been created. Around two-thirds of these are self-employed and possibly

disguised unemployment. Many are in poorly paid jobs, on zero-hour contracts or doing more than one part-time job, instead of good, secure employment.
- **National Debt** continues high. In April 2010, just before the Coalition Government was elected, it had risen to £960 billion, forecast to be £1.5tn five years later and at the year ending February 2015, was £1.469tn, which means the debt will have increased by just over 50%. Measuring debt as a proportion of gross domestic product (GDP), it had changed from 62% in April 2010 to 80% in February 2015 – an increase of about a third.
- **The deficit.** At the end of the financial year 2009, the deficit was almost £90bn. At the financial year end 2012, the total deficit was £121 billion. In 2010, George Osborne forecast that the deficit would fall to £40bn by 2015; instead, it was about £100bn.
- **Public spending.** He plans to cut the welfare budget by £21bn each year in order to reduce public spending to 35% of GDP. According to the Office for Budget Responsibility (OBR), that would be its lowest level for 80 years. Paul Johnson of the Institute for Fiscal Studies described this as *"on a colossal scale"*, changing the role of the state *"beyond recognition"*. It would take us back to the 1930s, when citizens could seek little support from the welfare state.
- **Household debt** as a share of total household incomes is down. But the ratio, around 140% of GDP, remains high by international standards. The OBR expects the ratio to start rising again, back up to pre-crisis levels, mainly because people are expected to start borrowing heavily again to buy expensive houses.

When interest rates rise, many will be vulnerable. The OBR predicts household debt to incomes, 170% in 2010, will increase to 184% by 2020.

- **Rebalancing the economy.** GDP growth in the second quarter of 2014 was 3.1% higher year on year but around 80% of this was the increase in services output. Services output is now 3% above its 2008 peak but manufacturing output is still over 7% below its level of six years ago, and construction is 11% per cent lower. Exports and business investment have fallen short of expectations.
- **GDP per capita.** GDP per capita is a better measure of national wellbeing than GDP. Although the economy is slightly bigger than six years ago, the population is considerably larger. So GDP per capita still languishes.
- **Real wage squeeze.** Wages in real terms are still considerably lower than in 2008. The median disposable income according to ONS figures is £500 less when inflation is taken into account. The cumulative loss is large.
- **Hidden unemployment.** Employment has held up surprisingly well since 2008; unemployment has fallen to 6.5%. More than 1.1 million new jobs have been created, despite the weak economy. Around two-thirds of these are self-employed positions, the quality of which is unclear; they could be disguised unemployment. Official surveys suggest considerable underemployment economy, with people saying they wish to work more hours than they have. Output per worker and per hour remains well below its 2008

level. Unless productivity improves, wages and living standards cannot rise.
- **The danger of another recession.** When the Bank of England starts to put up interest rates from the present low 0.5% (such a rate encourages borrowing, spending unsustainably, and feeds the housing bubble and the mad machine), as expected, around the turn of the year, the personal finances of some households could be badly hit. Then the danger is that people could stop spending, precipitating another recession.

For some of these figures, I thank Ben Chu: *"Government hails latest GDP figures, but there is still room for scepticism over this 'glorious recovery'."* The Independent, Saturday 26th July 2014 (www.independent.co.uk/voices/comment/government-hails-latest-gdp-figures-but-there-is-still-room-for-scepticism-over-this-glorious-recovery-9629812.html) and official figures

Again, I think of George Orwell's words quoted earlier:

*"Political language is designed to make lies sound truthful and murder respectable, and to give an appearance of solidity to pure wind."* **George Orwell** in **Why I Write – The English Revolution**

I return to Joseph Stiglitz:

*"If the facts don't fit the theory, change the theory, goes the old adage. But too often it is easier to keep the theory and change the facts – or so German Chancellor, Angela Merkel,*

*and other pro-austerity European leaders appear to believe. Though facts keep staring them in the face, they continue to deny reality. ... But every downturn comes to an end. Success should not be measured by the fact that recovery eventually occurs, but by how quickly it takes hold and how extensive the damage caused by the slump."* **Joseph E. Stiglitz**, author of *Europe's Austerity Disaster*, ex-Senior Vice President and Chief Economist of the World Bank (http://www.project-syndicate.org/commentary/joseph-e--stiglitz-wonders-why-eu-leaders-are-nursing-a-dead-theory).

*Mea culpa!* How refreshing it would be if we had more truthful political leaders. Surely they'd gain a landslide – especially if the media were equally truthful. But it would be very hard to admit such an enormous mistake.

***Many people tell me that they have given up watching or listening to the news.*** It's too depressing. The usual *Radio 4 Today*, *Newsnight* and Channel 4 formula is to get two adversaries to talk for a few minutes, expressing their opposing views, often interrupting each other. Then, *"I am sorry, we have run out of time."* – just at the point when we could be getting somewhere and probing deeper. Often, the listener is none the wiser. It is an entirely inadequate way of dealing with issues of great importance.

Newspapers, on the whole full of sensational stories and bad news, are likely to leave one feeling overwhelmed and powerless. *The Guardian* and *The Independent* are more positive. However, anyone wanting to be well-informed would go to the internet and find reliable sources. Positive News, owned by its readers, is dedicated to good news and inspiration (positivenews.org.uk/).

**the 21st century revolution**

## *Leadership is the big issue*

***The current qualifications for political leadership are not those required of effective stateswomen and statesmen***, capable of bold, long-term thinking and transformative leadership. They are those of the alpha male, quick to seize short-term party political advantage, and ministers like bulls in a china shop, imposing their pet views on our health services and schools without properly involving people on the ground, respected professional bodies, think tanks and research organisations. It's dangerous having such people in national leadership who don't know how to lead, and who are unaware of the ways in which they are illiterate.

***Lessons from the past three decades.*** I believe that as a result of the experiences of the last three decades, there is growing understanding of the need for radical **system change**; that treating symptoms doesn't work; that prevention is better and ultimately cheaper than cure (enormous suffering and cost could be saved in health, for example); we need heart as well as head; and we need holistic science. (www.plymouth.ac.uk/courses/postgraduate/msc-holistic-science)

***The need for courage and truth.*** Political leaders have not yet shown the courage to lead opinion, tell the truth about the dangerous situation we are in, and admit past mistakes. Blaming New Labour for the debt crisis is nonsense. The financial crisis began in the USA and was enabled by Neoliberal policies initiated by Ronald Reagan and Margaret Thatcher and continued under New Labour.

Labour should say so. Instead, leaders respond to the daily stories in the press with their eye on the next election.

It needs to be boldly said:
1. Austerity and cuts have failed and there will be no commitment to continuing this policy. Good housekeeping – yes.
2. Working in co-operation with other countries to address Climate Chaos is the top priority for humanity.
3. And it is our greatest opportunity to bring about prosperity and world peace.

We have seen the dangers posed by psychopathic and narcissistic leaders. Too often we are led by psychopaths and narcissists, charming but unscrupulous. Often, they lead us into disastrous wars. Who do you have in mind? (*Snakes in Suits: When Psychopaths Go to Work* by Paul Babiak and Robert Hare – www.psychologytoday.com/blog/wired-success/201312/why-are-there-more-psychopaths-in-the-boardroom.

Political leaders need to work for consensus with others so that the policies they implement, particularly expensive re-organisations, are not reversed when there is a change of power. Committed people who spend their lives in public service become disillusioned when all their work is thrown away when yet another re-organisation is introduced. Political leaders need to base their policies, not on ideology, but a rigorous enquiry into what will work. This requires harnessing the collective intelligence and creativity of all stakeholders, people from all party persuasions, especially people on the ground. They require the experience of excellent practitioners, professional bodies, and the research of relevant, genuinely independent think tanks such as the New Economics Foundation and Institute for Public Policy Research.

***We need transformative leaders who understand that they need to be hosts.*** Driving change is a false notion. Leaders need to understand how to bring about the co-creation of change with people of diverse views, representing all stakeholders. This releases human creativity, inspiring and engaging people in creating change, not by proposing and then consulting, but by involvement. The idea of *"getting the whole system into the room"* is vital if the best ways forward are to be discovered and people are to be whole-heartedly committed (*Creating the futures we desire – getting the whole system into the room* (www.brucenixon.com/writings3.html). Another invaluable approach is Consensus Design (www.christopherday.eu/).

Before taking office, political leaders should be required to take part in a top-quality leadership education programme including ecological science and how to involve and enable people in bringing about change. MPs should also be required to take part in a similar induction programme. This is best company practice for business leaders – why not?

***We need political leaders with stature:*** Mahatma Gandhi, Franklin D. Roosevelt, John Maynard Keynes, Winston Churchill, George C. Marshall, Clement Attlee and his colleagues, and Nelson Mandela. We need political leaders who think strategically and selflessly about our long-term future, and who inspire the nation.

**bruce nixon**

As I wrote in the Introduction, the nation faced a Nazi invasion, a complete takeover of Europe and world domination. What we are confronted with today is an even greater challenge: it is the greatest challenge in human history; the catastrophic effects of climate change and destruction of the ecological system. In 1940, the nation, with an incompetent government and military, and a dysfunctional industrial economy, faced invasion and defeat. The mass of people were disillusioned – much the same as today.

And we did triumph in a seemingly impossible situation. The nation and its remarkable leadership dared to be great. Winston Churchill's wartime national government with Clement Attlee as his deputy took over; the nation was inspired and we and the allies won the war. Clement Attlee won the post-war election and implemented a new social contract with overwhelming support. There is much to be learned from his approach to leadership. In particular, he did not interfere or constantly react to the media. Nicklaus Thomas-Symonds, author of a biography of Clement Attlee, offers a glimpse of the man who, for some, was the UK's greatest PM (*Total Politics* October 2012 –www.totalpolitics.com/commenting/post-comment.php#comments.

*"Some 37 years after his (Attlee's) death, in 2004, a poll of university academics rated Clement Attlee the 20$^{th}$ century's greatest prime minister... Winston Churchill was second... Attlee's greatness lay in getting the best out of other great men."*

## *Where will the new leadership come from?*

Where are people like this today? They are there. It is a different era, requiring a different kind of leadership. They are emerging; more will emerge as the public demand more of their leaders. Many more will be women, like Nicola Sturgeon, leader of the SNP, Leanne Wood of Plaid Cymru, and Natalie Bennett of the Greens, as we recognise the importance of the difference they offer. We need more politicians with real-life experience who seek service rather than power – servant leaders (The Greenleaf Centre for Servant-Leadership UK – www.greenleaf.org.uk/). We need them at the top of our great businesses too.

There will also be much more bottom-up leadership.

***More than ever, our survival depends on collaboration*** between people and nations in pursuit of the common good. This is embodied in the United Nations. There are already growing shortages of resources, land grabs and potential conflicts. Resolving these conflicts peacefully brings people together. Conflicts are rarely resolved through war. We know that respect for difference is vital; injustice breeds extremism and violence. Violence breeds more violence. Resolution of conflict through conciliation works (Chapter 8). There is the same need for a non-adversarial approach to politics. Instead, consensus building and shared power is required, as I shall argue in Chapter 9.

**bruce nixon**

## The state of democracy

***Widespread loss of confidence in our current democracy.*** Millions of people gave their lives fighting for democracy. Women were imprisoned and died fighting for their rights. But now, in the UK, there is widespread loss of confidence in the parliamentary democracy, fought so hard for by previous generations. People think there is little to choose between the main parties.

Not surprisingly, turnout on 22nd May 2014 for the European and local elections in the UK was only 36%. Across the EU, it was 43.11%. Over 6 million people in the UK were not registered to vote. In April 2015, 800,000 young Britons were missing from the voters' register. Compare these figures with the 84.59% turnout in the Scottish referendum, which included 16-17-year-olds, unlike UK elections.

***In the May 2015 election*** 61% voted. The results were: Conservative 331 seats, Labour 232, Scottish National Party 56, Liberal Democrat 8, Democratic Unionist Party 8, UKIP 1, The Green Party 1, others 13. UKIP and the Greens received five million votes – and got just two seats between them. The (pro-reform) SNP got around 1.5m votes and 56 seats, while the Democratic Unionist Party, with fewer than 200,000 votes, got the same number of MPs as the 2.5m vote-strong Lib Dems (main source: Electoral Reform Society (ERS)).

The good news is that 191 women were elected and female representation went up from 23% in the last Parliament to nearly 30%, putting us 36th in the world

## the 21st century revolution

rankings. Yet there's still a long way to go before equality, especially with "safe seats" being largely held by incumbent male MPs. A fair voting system would open these seats up to competition from people with more diverse backgrounds.

However, as the ERS points out, something is seriously wrong. Most people's votes were essentially wasted. Of the almost 31 million people who voted, 19 million voted for losing candidates. That's 63% of voters who backed a candidate that didn't win, making the vast majority of voters feel unrepresented. That doesn't sound like democracy to most people. The reverse of this is that many of the MPs who did win failed to get the support of most voters. Out of 650 winning candidates, 322 (49%) got less than 50% of the vote. With less than half the electorate backing them, that's a fairly weak mandate.

Under a fair voting system, such as the D'Hondt system of proportional representation, the election results would be: Conservatives 244 seats, Labour 201, UKIP 83 LibDem 52 SNP 31 Green 25, minor parties 14. Conservatives would still be the largest party, but 37% should never equal 51% of seats in a real democracy. It's a condemnation of the political class who have resisted reform of our democracy for so long.

Now the good news. It is not surprising that large numbers of people (74% of the British public) back a more proportional voting system. As I write, Unlock Democracy and the Electoral Reform Society had joined forces to demand a fairer, more proportional voting system, and 478,000 people had signed their petition before it was handed in to number 10 Downing Street (Electoral Reform Society:

http://electoral-reform.org.uk/press-release/party-leaders-unite-call-electoral-reform).

**The toxic, adversarial culture of the House of Commons is a huge turn-off.** People constantly tell me they are disgusted with the rowdy show at Prime Minister's Question Time. The two political leaders seemed unaware of how damaging this puerile behaviour is. They simply *"don't get it"*. It may bring cheers from their colleagues but it is a major turn-off. Party membership, once a source of identity for millions, is just over 1% of the population, low by European standards. There are more members of the Royal Society for the Protection of Birds (over 1 million) than of all Britain's political parties put together. Amongst the reasons for this is that the main political parties are out of date. Politicians seem unaware of how the public see them, so are obviously putting their political interests before those of the nation.

The behaviour of political leaders sets a bad example by blaming, not being truthful and not accepting responsibility; it's the behaviour of the school playground. It has disastrous effects when applied to violent conflicts such as those in Gaza and Israel, and in the Ukraine.

Some good members of Parliament, from both houses, have got out, as they believe they can do more outside of politics.

**An archaic anachronism.** The Parliament building (according to the Speaker, now needing £3bn to modernise and repair it), with its ancient ceremonies, is ridiculously anachronistic. This is no reflection on our Queen. How could any normal person work in such a place without being infected with hubris? The debating chamber in two opposing rows, supposedly separated by the distance between two swords, should be replaced with a consensus-building circle. The same applies to committee rooms. In a modern democracy, we need buildings that have chambers with seats arranged in a circle. It seems that many people felt much the same about Parliament in the 19th century. In his utopian novel, *News from Nowhere*, written in 1890, William Morris, describing London as it would be at about our time, said that the Parliament building had become a market for horse dung, perhaps reflecting much contemporary opinion.

**The traditional set-up of our politics and Parliament needs to be re-thought.** We urgently need creative solutions to our problems and ways forward that will work; these are not discovered in an atmosphere of **opposition** – that description of the foolish, out-dated role of parties not in government – attacking each other and wanting to be right. The solution of the major challenges we face requires an open mind, a willingness to learn, and building consensus together on ways forward. The cross-party committees of the House of Commons provide a better model.

**Corrupted democracy.** In his article, *The Real Power in Politics* in *Resurgence & Ecologist*, March 2014, Donnachadh McCarthy argues that our state has four distinct pillars: a corrupted democracy, a captured media, a hijacked academia, and a criminal tax-haven system.

He quotes this example:
*"Despite the public's favouring renewable power over nuclear by a large margin, all three main parties are now committed to pouring up to £420 billion into yet more nuclear behemoths, instead of investing this money in making poorer households energy-efficient and freeing them from exorbitant energy bills."*

He attributes this to undisclosed corporate lobbyists' infiltration of the state and influencing politicians. The *"revolving door"* between business and government prejudices the state mind-set and damages independence of thought. Moving people between roles as legislators and regulators, and the industries concerned, is likely to compromise legislation and regulation.

According to an article in *The Observer*, 46% of top firms in UK had a Parliamentarian, either as a director or shareholder. A former boss of HMRC took up a job with Deloitte, who advise clients on minimising tax. Over the past decade, 18 ex-ministers and former civil servants ended up working for the big four accountancy firms (*The Establishment: And How They Get Away With It*: John Kampfner, *The Observer*, 31st August 2014).

There is increasing corporate domination of our education system, undermining crucial freedom of thought, including primary and secondary schools, universities and university research. The three main political parties are dependent on funding from tax-haven associated companies and millionaire donors. UK tax-havens are being used to shift the tax burden from corporations to the ordinary citizen, thus contributing to the public sector deficit. They are

## the 21st century revolution

also the route by which the wealth of poorest nations is funnelled into Western banks.

For democracy to work, citizens must be well-informed. That is far from being the case. The nation is subjected to daily propaganda. Donnachadh McCarthy reveals that five tax-avoiding billionaires control over 80% of UK daily newspapers; 18% of the rest is largely in the hands of international financial corporations, leaving only *The Guardian* at 2.6% to represent the interests of the non-billionaire section of society (*The Mirror* still supports Labour however). These five billionaires also own a significant proportion of our TV, film and book industries, thus exerting an iron grip on vast swathes of British culture. We need measures, stronger than the Independent Press Standards Organisation (IPSO), which enables readers to challenge editors or journalists who mislead us with false facts on vital issues such as climate change, and if proved guilty, to be required to apologise, pay a penalty or be struck off.

Murdoch (*The Sun/The Times*), Desmond (*The Express*), Rothermere (*The Mail*), and the Barclay Brothers (*The Telegraph*) monopolise our media. If this continues, we'll never create the social and environmental justice that so many of us dream of and work so hard for. However, the good news is that this media is on its way out; younger people find their information on the internet. *The Independent*, founded by Anreas Whittam Smith, is owned by former billionaire, Alexander Lebedev. It is centre-left on culture and politics, but tends to be pro-market on economic issues. It features a range of views given on its editorial and comment pages. The paper originally described itself

**bruce nixon**

as *"free from party political bias, free from proprietorial influence"* – a banner it carried on the front page of its daily edition. This was dropped in September 2011.

Donnachadh McCarthy argues that so long as the ultra-rich control the production of thought, the dissemination of thought, the implementation of thought, and the funding of thought, then we no longer live in a democracy but in a *Prostitute State*, the title of his new book (www.theprostitutestate.co.uk/page2.html).

***A Great Democratic Reform Act.*** Donnachadh McCarthy urges us, civic society, the National Trust, trade unions, churches, and credit unions to call for a 21st century Great Democratic Reform Act, as they did in the 19th century, when popular pressure from the people overcame the entrenched aristocracy through the Reform Acts.

Under such an act, politicians would be barred from becoming lobbyists, our Fourth Estate (i.e. news media) would be reclaimed, academia freed from corporate interference, and tax-havens closed. Global environmental catastrophes and the ever-increasing erosion of social justice are in danger of overwhelming us if we do not act. Donnachadh McCarthy says the captured media must be our first target. Our futures should not be held hostage to the financial interests of the ultra-rich. Without this pillar, the other pillars will crumble. He urges us to join work together for reform. (Thanks to Donnachadh McCarthy, writing in Resurgence – www.resurgence.org/magazine/article4105-the-real-power-in-politics.html)

### the 21st century revolution

***Here is the danger.*** Despite our concerns and discontent, many of us believe we have only enough time and energy to earn a living and care for our family; they feel stretched to the limit. Some feel tired and depressed – two things that go together – and their energy is sapped. *"We don't have time to be activists. There is no point anyway; things can't be changed."* This is a self-fulfilling prophesy. But if we decide to live lightly on our planet, we'll have more time for all the joys of family life, the natural beauty that surrounds us, and time to be activists.

*"Activism is my rent for living on the planet."* **Alice Walker**

**So what do we need to do to break corporate power and create truly representative government?** There are 7bn of us; we have far greater power if we use it. We can shame corporations that abuse their power; we can withhold our purchasing power; we can divest; we can protest and petition; we can simply use our influence; we can put forward positive proposals of which there is no shortage. Coalitions of think tanks are more effective than when they act singly.

# Chapter 2

# *The multiple challenges we face*

*"In this system, which tends to devour everything which stands in the way of accrued profits, whatever is fragile like the environment is defenceless against the interest of a deified market, which becomes the only rule."* **Pope Francis**

## *Destruction of our habitat*

The current version of capitalism is driving us to the brink of environmental catastrophe and creating an increasingly unjust and divided world.

***We live on a beautiful planet, perfectly suited to our needs.*** Over the millennia, perfect conditions were created for human life. It could be a paradise. Yet we are destroying it. Everyone could have the opportunity for a happy, fulfilling life; we have the means as never before. The planet is abundant – there's enough for everyone – it is a matter of how we husband and share this abundance. Nature will provide us with what we need but only if we respect her and each other. We constantly do otherwise and we may already have gone too far. The Green Revolution, involving agrichemicals, like so many other experiments with nature, had unintended consequences. Now the potential consequences are far worse.

***Destruction of forests and loss of species.*** We are rapidly destroying forests, despite knowing their importance, and polluting the seas with plastic debris. In his TED Talk, Patrick Alley, director of Global Compass, spoke about the scandal of the rapid destruction of the world's forests by greedy, corrupt businessmen and politicians. They are the lungs of the planet; they are crucial in regulating our water and climate systems, home to one in six human beings, half of the world's animals and plant species. An article in the *Ethical Consumer*, August 2014, says we cannot rely on the Forest Stewardship Council (FSC) certification because auditing companies are not dependable. Many species are in rapid decline and in danger of extinction. The London Zoological Society in its new *Living Planet Index* says species populations have halved in the past 40 years.

Mammals, birds, reptiles, amphibians and fish have declined by an average of 52%. In the UK, 60% of our wildlife species and over 50% of farmland birds are in decline; there are 50% fewer hedgehogs than 25 years ago, and 10% of wildlife species face extinction. Bees, vital for our crops, are in decline. Neonicotinoids are up to 10,000 more toxic to bees than DDT. The Soil Association is appealing for funds to fight for a permanent ban on their use.

Scientists tell us that Earth has entered its sixth mass extinction, the worst level for 66 million years, with animals dying out at 100 times the normal rate. We have created a toxic mix of habitat loss, pollution and climate change, leading to the loss of at least 77 (26%) species of mammals,

140 (12%) types of birds and 34 (41%) amphibians since 1500 (Stanford Report, June 19th, 2015 news.stanford.edu/news/2015/june/mass-extinction-ehrlich-061915.html).

We know the importance of diversity yet we are destroying it. Agribusiness depends on just a few varieties of vegetables, and the EU limits seed varieties through an expensive system of seed registration that it is now trying to extend.

***Soil.*** A healthy soil containing millions of creatures is essential to our existence. Soils are home to a quarter of all known living species. Yet agrichemicals destroy them and our soil is degrading faster than nature can restore it. As a result of intense farming in the UK, we have lost 84% of our fertile top soils since 1850. Water scarcity, flooding, soil erosion and heat are the four greatest risk factors. Erosion is continuing at a rate of one to three centimetres per year. Yet we are paving our gardens, destroying woodland, and building on countryside, all increasing the risk of flooding. Organic farmers are a declining species for want of support. Increasingly, we import organic food when we need to be more self-sufficient (Committee on Climate Change (CCC) report: www.theccc.org.uk).

It's madness. Why can't we understand that we are part of nature and we must live in harmony with it to survive? Instead of nature being part of our lives, it's something we watch on TV and consign to nature reserves and museums. 98% of England's once abundant flower meadows have been destroyed since the 1930s. It is common sense that we cannot master nature. Not only are we at war with

## the 21st century revolution

nature but we are at war with each other when, to save ourselves from annihilation, we need to collaborate.

***We're warming up the planet and getting fatter.*** Professor Ian Roberts explains the simple link between the two in his book, *The Energy Glut*. We're warming up the planet and getting fatter and unhealthier, sitting in ever bigger cars and at computers, instead of walking and cycling (www.youtube.com/watch?v=tjPA_dlXoVM). We're eating more energy than we burn up and it's the wrong food. So 25% of us are obese, 64% overweight in UK, costing the NHS half its budget. Air pollution causes 29,000 early deaths a year in the UK – more than obesity and alcohol combined – and the UK is breaking air pollution laws (ClientEarth www.clientearth.org/news/press-releases/supreme-court-rules-uk-government-is-breaking-air-pollution-laws-2170). Under the terms of an EU directive on dirty air, the UK fails to meet the standards required in 34 of the country's 43 zones. London and two other regions would not meet the legal limits until 2030. In London, it is estimated that almost 9% of deaths or some 4,000 early deaths are caused by air pollution. Nitrogen dioxide, mainly from diesel engines, is particularly harmful.

*"A whole generation of young people in our cities will potentially have their health impaired by pollution before the Government meets air quality safety standards."* **Joan Walley, Chair of the Environmental Audit Committee (EAC)**

Sugar consumption is another factor. Sugary drinks are killing 184,000 adults around the world every year (www.

nhs.uk/news/2015/06June/Pages/Sugary-drinks-killing-hundreds-of-thousands-claims-study.aspx).

Given these conditions, the lack of health education early in life and the unavailability of therapies for ordinary working people that would prevent physical deterioration, it is not surprising that the NHS faces escalating demands and ever-increasing costs. Corporations responsible for these harms should change their ways or be taxed upstream to provide the necessary finance.

There is better news on this subject in Chapter 3.

Because of greed, wanting to dominate, and a short-sighted mind-set, we are steadily heating up and destroying our habitat. Not content with that, we are now looking to exploit the deep seas and even seeking other planets to exploit or escape to. We hardly begin to understand the complexity of the ecosystem on which our lives and all other life depends. Where is our humility in the face of this wonder? In the name of "science", a science that is not holistic and often not independent, we poison the soil, making it a lifeless medium for agrochemicals; we are killing other forms of life, calling them pests or weeds.

**Unlike Lucida, our honest hunter cat** – she goes out, kills and eats her dinner – we buy our meat in nice packets with little idea of how the animals may have suffered in the process. In large-scale, industrialised farming, we treat animals with horrifying cruelty but keep that well out of sight.

the 21st century revolution

## *Feeding the world*

**The UN says there is enough food in the world** to feed everyone, even if the population expands to 9bn by mid-century (it is likely to decline after that). GM Freeze say there is enough food in the world to feed 14bn. The problem is how it is distributed. Some of us have too much and waste half of it; others do not have enough or are starving. Half the population of the world are farmers. When they are tricked out of their land, they end up in cities living in dire conditions. By taking their land away, getting them into debt by miss-selling GM crops and herbicides, or paying them too little, as we do in UK, we are forcing them out. Industrial scale agribusiness is taking over. Is food production safe in their hands? Can we trust them? Judging from the record of Big Business, persisting in selling us unhealthy food, drinks and tobacco, we must doubt it. Agribusiness is unsustainable. More and more, we'll need local food as oil runs out and the climate becomes more chaotic.

*Farmers are an endangered species.* Small farmers provide 70% of the world's food and the principal employment in poorer countries. Yet they are under attack from Western development policies, principally designed to supply rich countries at their expense, and transnational agribusiness. In Britain, our farmers are also endangered. They are being forced to sell their cows. Dairy processors are offering them unsustainable prices. The average cost of production of a litre of milk is just over 30p. The typical price paid is now around 28p, down from around 35p in April. More cuts are predicted. This is an example of the cost of cheaper and cheaper prices in a free market. We are losing our food sovereignty and security at a time when it will be most needed.

**Supermarkets** are part of the problem, as many of us know. They have helped create *Ghost Town Britain* ([www.neweconomics.org/publications/entry/ghost-town-britain](www.neweconomics.org/publications/entry/ghost-town-britain)) and they have contributed to the demise of many farmers and local high street shops. They have played their part in creating a nation of obese and overweight people, and shortening their lives. They have encouraged people to buy more than they need and, in various other ways, created an enormous waste of food. But the public are changing their buying habits and many regret the loss of local shops. They realise their importance to community. They are becoming much more aware and finding alternatives in local and farmers' markets. They realise the unsustainability of the food distribution system and the cost and unsustainability of driving rather than walking to local shops.

**Patterns of shopping are changing.** People are returning to shopping locally; street markets and farmers' markets are growing; some are turning to the internet to get their food and groceries delivered. Suddenly, the mighty supermarkets like Tesco, whose share price is plummeting, are facing falling sales and profits. Aldi and Lidl are giving them a run for their money. Even Walmart has had to cut its profit forecasts. In her article, *Why supermarkets are on the way out*, in *The Guardian*, 7th October 2014, Felicity Lawrence says:

## the 21st century revolution

*"The fall of empire, when it does come, tends to be fast, the seeds of decline obvious in retrospect."*

We may find this will also prove true for Big Oil, Big Gas, Big Banks, Big Agribusiness, Neoliberal economics and austerity too.

**Big companies, backed by captive scientists and governments, are carrying out dangerous experiments with our planet without our consent, and often without our knowledge.** Read GM Freeze (www.gmfreeze.org/) for a full understanding of the crop failures, harms and dangers of GM seeds, coupled with pesticides sold by companies like Cargill, Monsanto and Syngenta, and their biopiracy, i.e. patenting of natural food crops. Amongst the key issues are:

1. There is no effective way of preventing GM crops contaminating non-GM and organic crops.
2. There is a lack of evidence that GM crops are NOT harmful to human health. This is not possible in the USA where GM food products are not labelled.
3. The most common type of GM crop is designed to be heavily sprayed with glyphosate, which the World Health Organisation recently classified as probably causing cancer.
4. GM crops have so far failed to deliver any of the promised benefits.
5. Small farmers in countries like India have got severely in debt – many committing suicide.
6. Do we really want a handful of transnational agribusinesses – Cargill and Monsanto – to dominate world food? Is it wise to rely on a small number of

> seed varieties? What is needed is diversity to suit different conditions.
> 7. So why incur the unknown risks involved in GM when uncontroversial, agro-ecologic crops can improve yields and resistance to draught and disease.

***GM is no answer to feeding the world.*** These companies are doing great harm to small and medium-sized farmers who know how to grow food crops adapted to local conditions. We need agro-ecologic food production, not industrialised agribusiness. There is outrage in many countries including the USA – see Nation of Change (www.nationofchange.org/) and GM Freeze (www.gmfreeze.org/). Yet Britain's government is one of the strongest opponents of EU legislation to protect us from these harms. Once again, I say we are confronted with illiterate government.

### *Mind-set*

*"I fear it is not lack of information from our side that's the problem, it's a mind-set – they hear what they want to hear, they believe in high-tech (and often expensive and big technology) to solve problems – low-tech, often more complex (systems like organic as opposed to 'insert a gene and save the world') solutions just do not compute!"* **Peter Melchett**, Policy Adviser, Soil Association

And as **Eve Mitchell**, Food Rights Campaigner, says:

*"There are more of us than there are of them."*

## the 21st century revolution

"*Science says*", that beguiling phrase, is often used to tell us what the solution is – like GM crops and factory farming. It's another big *"con"*, another form of illiteracy amongst otherwise very clever people. The problem is that it is not **holistic** science.

*"Holistic science advocates a participatory science of qualities, values and interactions, which underpins an ecological world view. This approach is more capable than traditional science of relating to the problems of environmental degradation, spiritual decline and collapsing communities that face humanity today.* (Schumacher College)

**Wake up before it is too late.** The UN Commission on Trade and Development (UNCTAD) says the world can feed itself, but says transformative changes are needed in our food, agriculture and trade systems in order to increase diversity on farms, reduce our use of fertilizer and other inputs, support small-scale farmers, and create strong, local food systems. The report, *Trade and Environment Review 2013: Wake Up Before it is Too Late*, included contributions from over 60 experts around the world. A shift is needed toward more sustainable, resilient agriculture, livestock production, land use; and the reform of global trade rules. It links global security and escalating conflicts with the urgent need to transform agriculture toward what it calls *"ecological intensification"*. It concludes:

*"This implies a rapid and significant shift from conventional, monoculture-based and high-external-input-dependent industrial production toward mosaics of sustainable, regenerative production systems that also considerably improve the productivity of small-scale farmers."* **Ben**

**Lilliston**, Institute for Agriculture and Trade Policy (IATP), September 20th, 2013 (www.iatp.org/blog/201309/new-un-report-calls-for-transformation-in-agriculture)

This was the opposite of UK's Coalition policy. International development, as practised by countries like the UK, means *"all roads lead to the ports"*. Instead of helping the development of the local economy by, for instance, providing people with bicycles that make an enormous difference to their lives, the beneficiaries are big companies, big banks, consumers in rich countries and corrupt politicians. This form of aid increases indebtedness and robs taxpayers. Grants should be given instead. The wealth within poorer countries largely goes to a few rich people and corrupt politicians. Much of this trade also undercuts UK providers and puts them out of business. The large amount of transport involved is an additional cause of climate change and ill health (*The health co-benefits of climate change policies* – www.clinmed.rcpjournal.org/content/9/3/212.full.pdfwww.wdm.org.uk/injuryprevention.bmj.com/content/10/2/65.full).

**The EU/US Transatlantic Trade and Investment Partnership (TTIP) Deal is a serious threat to democracy.** Here is a typical example of how corporations, without most of us knowing, are being enabled to abuse their power. Current negotiations on this new deal, called the Investor State Dispute Settlement mechanism (ISDS) will, if allowed by us citizens, give corporations new rights to sue governments of countries directly for laws or acts that have an adverse effect on their ability to make money without any democratic oversight or resource. So, for example, Monsanto could sue the French government for a renewed ban on GM Maize. If passed, this agreement will affect the ability of our democratically-elected representatives to make laws to protect us citizens from the damaging effects of unaccountable corporations. That is one of the key roles of governments. It means putting profit and shareholders before the interests of people. It threatens all public services, our health services and education, food safety, climate change efforts, our democracy, reform of banking and much more. To prevent this threat to democracy, go to Stop TTIP (www.stopttip.net/) and the 38 Degrees Campaign against TTIP (www.38degrees.org.uk/).

**The G7's New Alliance for Food Security and Nutrition** of big companies, including Coca-Cola, Diageo and Unilever, threatens to take power over food production in Africa. 70% of Africa's food is produced by small-scale farmers. Big companies would force farmers to grow export crops, meeting the needs of big companies, instead of focussing on sustainable, small-scale production to meet the needs of local people. How can it be stopped? The first step would be for the UK government to stop channelling £600m of UK aid money through the New Alliance. Instead, UK aid should be used to support the policies that promote food sovereignty. This would enable small farmers to maintain control over their resources to produce food sustainably and prioritise food for local populations over exports. (See more at: www.wdm.org.uk/food/about-the-campaign#sthash.hh5EHcyn.dpuf).

**bruce nixon**

# Economic and social injustice – Growing inequality and poverty

*"An economic system that fails to deliver gains for most of its citizens is a failed economic system."* **Joseph Stiglitz**, former World Bank Chief Economist

***Multidimensional Poverty.*** 1.6 billion people live in "multidimensional poverty". No one indicator, such as income, can capture the multiple aspects that constitute poverty. Multidimensional poverty is made up of several factors that constitute poor people's experience of deprivation – such as poor health, lack of education, inadequate nutrition, living standard, disempowerment, poor quality of work and threat from violence. This approach reveals that the number living in poverty is twice those living on $1.25 a day, and two-thirds of such people live in middle-income countries (thanks to Oxford Poverty & Human Development Initiative (OPHI) – www.ophi.org.uk).

***We're all colonised now.*** Until now, colonisation was something the West inflicted on other races, the so-called Third World. Trickle-down is a myth; it's trickle-up! In the world, the division into rich and poor is even greater and steadily growing. Rich nations are responsible for enormous levels of exploitation. Slavery was justified on the idea that black people are not human, or not as human as white people. A different form of slavery is now as widespread as ever. Today, small children work in the most appalling conditions with their mothers on waste heaps of rubbish exported by rich nations like ours; we know about the bad and unsafe conditions in factories making cheap products for us. We prefer not to address the underlying system that causes exploitation and poverty; instead, whilst continuing to enjoy an affluent life, we salve our consciences with charity.

A UK Slavery Bill gained Royal Assent on 26th March, 2015. Modern slavery affects more than 35 million people. Five countries, including India, China and Russia, account for 61% of all slavery, says the Walk Free Foundation. People of all religions are now uniting in the Global Freedom Network to put an end to slavery (www.globalfreedomnetwork.org).

**The good news is that students all over the world are demanding that economics teaching be reformed**. The International Student Initiative for Pluralist Economics (ISIPE) (www.isipe.net) argues that economics courses are failing wider society when they ignore evidence from other disciplines; the research and teaching in economics departments is too narrowly-focussed and more effort should be made to broaden the curriculum. They want courses to include analysis of the financial crash that so many economists failed to see coming, and the teaching of economics has become divorced from the real world. I quote from their open letter:

*"It is not only the world economy that is in crisis. The teaching of economics is in crisis too, and this crisis has consequences far beyond the university walls. What is taught shapes the minds of the next generation of policymakers, and therefore shapes the societies we live in. We, over 65 associations of economics students from over 30 different countries, believe it is time to reconsider the way economics is taught. We are*

### bruce nixon

*dissatisfied with the dramatic narrowing of the curriculum that has taken place over the last couple of decades. This lack of intellectual diversity does not only restrain education and research. It limits our ability to contend with the multidimensional challenges of the 21$^{st}$ century – from financial stability to food security and climate change. The real world should be brought back into the classroom, as well as debate and a pluralism of theories and methods. Such change will help renew the discipline and ultimately create a space in which solutions to society's problems can be generated."*

**Rethinking Economics** is another organisation challenging current orthodoxy. It is an international network of students, thinkers and citizens, coming together to demystify, diversify, invigorate economics, and to promote a politics of responsibility (www.rethinkeconomics.org).

***Diversity is nature's way.*** Diversity enhances our chances of survival; it is also a source of creativity and cultural richness. Exploitation of other human beings, overconsumption, competition for the Earth's resources and intolerance are at the root of wars, civil wars and violence. The daily news brings us the dreadful stories of massacres, fleeing migrants drowning in the Mediterranean, millions killed or seriously injured, families displaced from their homes and countries, children traumatised, and soldiers broken by their experiences. Their number grows. All this has been so throughout human history. It is time to see sense and give it up. Furthermore, countries like the UK continue to profit from manufacturing and selling armaments. Instead, we should invest in creating a zero-carbon Britain, making our country energy efficient, and promoting peace and reconciliation (www.peacedirect.org/us).

**Yet many of us are intolerant of diversity.** Nearly a third of people in Britain admit to being racially-prejudiced, according to recent research. In a recent survey by NatCen, 30% of those polled described themselves as either *"very"* or *"a little"* race-prejudiced, compared with an all-time low of 25% of people in 2001. The British Social Attitudes survey found the proportion had increased since the start of the century, returning to the level of 30 years ago.

*"No one is born hating another person because of the colour of his skin, or his background, or his religion. People must learn to hate, and if they can learn to hate, they can be taught to love, for love comes more naturally to the human heart than its opposite."* **Nelson Mandela**

**Almost half of the world's wealth is now owned by just 1% of the population**, Oxfam says, and seven out of ten people live in countries where economic inequality has increased in the last thirty years. The 85 richest people in the world have more than the poorest 3.5bn; 1% own half the world's wealth; tax dodging costs poor countries $160bn; the number of billionaires has doubled to 1,646 since the financial crisis hit hard in 2009, and any return to growth is *"not being shared with the vast majority"*. Since 2009, one million women have died in childbirth for lack of basic healthcare, and 58 million children are denied education (www.oxfam.org/en/research/time-end-extreme-inequality).

**bruce nixon**

The World Economic Forum has identified economic inequality as a major risk to human progress, impacting social stability within countries and threatening security on a global scale. This massive concentration of economic resources in the hands of fewer people presents a real threat to inclusive political and economic systems. And it compounds other inequalities – such as those between women and men. Left unchecked, political institutions are undermined and governments overwhelmingly serve the interests of economic elites – to the detriment of ordinary people.

Poverty is the main cause of disease outbreaks like Ebola, which spread and spread for lack of medical resources, and may become a massive threat to us all. This demonstrates how ending poverty, a moral responsibility, is in the interests of the whole world. Morality is long-term self-interest. Whatever happened to enlightened self-interest?

**Reducing income inequality would boost economic growth.** According to a new OECD analysis, countries where income inequality is decreasing grow faster than those with rising inequality. Incidentally, in Chapter 6, I shall be arguing that continuous growth is unsustainable and we need a better measure of prosperity than growth. Unfortunately, the UK has become one of the most unequal countries in the world, with very high levels of inequality between different regions (*Inequality Briefing* – inequalitybriefing.org). The single biggest impact on growth is the widening gap between the lower middle-class and poor households compared to the rest of society. Education is the key: a lack of investment in education by the poor is the main factor behind inequality hurting growth.

### the 21st century revolution

*"This compelling evidence proves that addressing high and growing inequality is critical to promote strong and sustained growth and needs to be at the centre of the policy debate. Countries that promote equal opportunity for all from an early age are those that will grow and prosper."*
**Angel Gurría**, OECD Secretary-General, *Trends in Income Inequality and its Impact on Economic Growth* (www.oecd.org/newsroom/inequality-hurts-economic-growth.htm)

***Debt is a major contributor to poverty and disease.***
Loans to poorer countries made by the World Bank and International Monetary Fund have left a legacy of crippling debt repayments and interest (Global Issues – www.globalissues.org). Often the developments they fund do not benefit the population and the economic gains go into the pockets of corrupt politicians. The main gains are for developed countries and big business. Vulture Funds are a particularly nasty feature: they buy up debt for very small sums and then sue the governments for repayment. One example is Argentina. Two US vulture funds have been trying to extract $1.3bn from Argentina but the US Supreme Court turned down Argentina's appeal. The United Nations General Assembly has passed a resolution to create new legal rules to stop financial speculators like vulture funds from undermining debt restructurings. The motion, passed by 124 votes to 11, has decided that the UN will create *"a multilateral legal framework for the sovereign debt restructuring processes"*. At present, there are no rules regarding how to restructure the debts of countries when they can no longer be paid, leading to prolonged debt crises and expensive bank bailouts, and an open door for vulture funds' extortion of countries in debt crisis. Britain and USA have opposed such measures. We need to learn

that grants, not loans, are the answer. Go to the Jubilee Debt Campaign (jubileedebt.org.uk/news/un-votes-rules-stop-vulture-funds) if you wish to support Argentina's campaign. Europe too needs to learn that defaulting on debt may be the best solution in some circumstances.

***Extreme inequality is not inevitable.*** In its report, *Working for the Few*, Oxfam shows how extreme inequality is not inevitable, with examples of policies from around the world that have reduced inequality and developed more representative politics, benefitting all, both rich and poor. Oxfam called on leaders at the 2014 World Economic Forum at Davos to make the commitments needed to counter the growing tide of inequality. (Source: Oxfam – www.oxfam.org/en/policy/working-for-the-few-economic-inequality Working for the Few: Political capture and economic inequality (summary))

## *A divided nation in a divided world*

In the UK, the Neoliberal (Neoliberalism is explained in Chapter 5) policies are creating extreme and growing levels of inequality and poverty, reminiscent of Victorian times. We're a divided nation in a divided world: divided between North and South, old and young but, above all, by rich and poor. Make no mistake; the rich are robbing us, the poor and now the middle-class. London is one of the most divided cities; the poorest and the richest extremes are growing. In London, about 36% households are now classified as poor, up from 20% in 1980, and 37% are middle income, down from 65% in 1980 (**Benjamin Hennig** and **Danny Dorling**, School of the Environment at Oxford University – www.londonmapper.org.uk/analysis/poverty-and-wealth-1980-2010).

Over the period of 1980 to 2010, there has been an 80% increase in poor households and an 80% increase in wealthy ones, and a 43% decrease in middle-class households. The rich have become 64% richer and the poor, 57% poorer. Recovery is likely to increase this divide (Social Market Foundation – www.smf.co.uk). By March 2014, the wealth of Britain's richest 1,000 people had risen from £258bn to £519bn, double the figure for 2009, and equivalent to a third of the nation's economic output (*Sunday Times Rich List*).

Middle-class Londoners are moving out of London, which has become a property haven for the super-rich. Again, the people who create the wealth, the goods and services that make our society work, are being impoverished. And this robbery grows day by day. It takes place in many ways: tax avoidance, regressive taxes, privatisation – selling state assets at knockdown prices, devices like Public Finance Initiatives, the power of the banks, bailing them out, low wages subsidised by the taxpayer and more.

**Poverty and inequality in UK.** 4.8 million UK workers, equivalent to 20% of employees, now earn below the so-called living wage, up from 3.4 million in 2009 (Resolution Foundation). Just over half of the 13 million people in poverty – surviving on less than 60% of the national median (middle) income – were from working families. The Joseph Rowntree Foundation says low pay and part-time work had prompted an unprecedented fall in living standards. More than 8 million people are now working part-time, almost

**bruce nixon**

75% women, not necessarily a bad thing, but part-time workers earn 36% less than full-time workers per hour.

There are 1.4 million people working on zero-hours contracts – *"contracts without guaranteed hours"* (Office for National Statistics). Many more people are working freelance; not necessarily earning much. There is a high level of insecurity. Being in employment is no guarantee of being able to put enough food on the table. According to the British Heart Foundation, high food prices mean a third of UK adults are struggling to afford to eat healthily and buy fresh fruit and vegetables. According to their poll of 2,444 adults, 39% sacrifice health benefits for cost when doing their grocery shopping.

***The unemployed and people on low wages are in dire straits.*** Personal debt is rising. Austerity and cuts have not reduced the rising National Debt – now £1.36 trillion (July 2015). The 400% growth in the use of food banks and 900,000 people dependent on them for survival in the world's sixth wealthiest country (GDP) is a shocking sign of the times.

***Young people are hard hit.*** One in three young workers, almost 1.5m, is on low pay. In 1975, the proportion was less than one in ten or 8% (Resolution Foundation). The real wages of 18-25-year-olds has fallen by 14% and 25-29-year-olds by 12% since the financial crisis in 2008. Many turned to payday lenders with dire consequences. Household incomes of under-30s are down 15%; large numbers are locked out of the housing market and live in shared housing, even shared rooms (Institute for Fiscal Studies). OECD has warned that millions of young people will struggle to fulfil their ambitions (Organisation for Economic Co-operation and Development – www.oecdbetterlifeindex.org).

**Wasted talent.** All this amounts to a colossal and needless waste of talent when, in reality, there is plenty of work to be done. It also carries a risk of widespread alienation and potential civil unrest.

Poverty and Social Exclusion (PSE)'s report, *The Impoverishment of the UK* (June 2014), revealed that over 30 million people (almost half the population) are suffering some degree of financial insecurity:
- Almost 12 million people are too poor to engage in common social activities considered necessary by the majority of the population.
- Around 4 million children and adults are not properly fed by today's standards.
- Around 2.5 million children live in homes that are damp.
- Around 1.5 million children live in households that cannot afford to heat their home.

**Child poverty.** Save the Children's recent report, *A Fair Start for Every Child*, said 5 million children in Britain could be *"sentenced to a lifetime of poverty"* by 2020 because of welfare reforms. Cuts to benefits, the rising cost of living, and years of flat wages have created a *"triple whammy"* for children. Children have borne the brunt of the recession in Britain, and now represent the *"face of poverty"* in the UK. Policies such as the *"bedroom tax"*, the slashing of tax credits and council tax relief, mean *"the social safety net no longer acts as a sufficient backstop for poor families"*. Soaring food prices and childcare costs have also hit families, the cost of food rising by 19% between 2007 and 2011. A nursery place for a child under two cost 77% more last year than 10 years ago. A significant proportion of families – as high as 28% in London – are skipping meals in a bid to make ends meet. In many areas, more than one in ten families cannot afford to buy children new shoes when they need them. Half of low-income families have seen their incomes decrease in the past five years. Around 70% had found it difficult to meet payments, and more than two in five said they had got into debt as a result. Political promises to eradicate child poverty by 2020 are *"no longer credible"*, the report says. It predicted the number of children living in poverty could rise by 1.4 million by 2020 – an increase of 41% on the current 3.5 million.

Without *"dramatic change"*, we risk *"writing off the future of millions of British children, giving them an unfair start in life"*, warned Justin Forsyth, Chief Executive of Save the Children. *"Far too many of our children are living in cold and damp homes, without healthy food, with parents who can see no end to their situation."* Work *"has ceased to become a sufficient solution to poverty for families with children"*, the report warns. Two-thirds of children in poverty now live in working households, a rise of 20% since 2003. The report added:

*"The UK remains one of the most unfair countries in the developed world – the lottery of birth still determines millions of children's chances in life."*

By 2020, child poverty could *"be around the highest ever recorded in the UK... the highest for a generation. The face*

## the 21st century revolution

*of poverty in the UK will be that of a child, usually within a working family."*

The Institute for Fiscal Studies (IFS) says their studies suggest that progress made in reducing child poverty between the 90s and 2010 has been reversed, and 2.6 million children live in relative poverty as of 2014. Factors contributing to this situation include the bedroom tax, delays in implementing Universal Credit, and expensive and poor quality childcare, which prevents some mothers working. The Child Poverty Action Group say that with the Government committed to £12bn cuts a year, the problem will grow, and they expect child poverty to grow by almost a third by 2020.

**A minimum income guarantee** is recommended by Save the Children for families with young children, high-quality and affordable childcare, and a mission to ensure all children are reading well by the age of 11. The minimum income in London needs to be the highest; and in big cities, it needs to be higher than in the nation as a whole.

**The prevailing mind-set of government** is the Neoliberal belief in free market economics, a limited concept of *"science"*, and big solutions imposed from the top, as opposed to small, holistic solutions created by communities and individuals. A bastion of Neoliberalism and a powerful obstacle to change is said to be HM Treasury. It starved British Rail of investment.

So we lost our lead in developing high-speed trains. More recently, the newly-created Green Investment Bank was castrated by totally inadequate funding and very limited borrowing capacity.

This mind-set needs to be replaced. I describe alternatives to these policies in Chapters 6 and 7.

**Prisons.** We put too many people in prison and we don't do enough to rehabilitate prisoners. Reformers have been saying this for many decades.

A report by the Prison Reform Trust (PRT) describes a deteriorating situation in prisons as a result of cuts. 1,575 serious assaults took place in prisons last year, the highest number for a decade, and a rise of more than 300 over the previous 12 months. 23,183 incidents of self-harm were recorded among inmates, a slight increase on the previous year. In the year to March 2014, 88 people committed suicide in prisons throughout England and Wales – a startling rise of 41 % on the previous 12 months. In 2013, there were 215 deaths in custody, the highest on record. The jail population was 84,305, an increase of more than 500. England and Wales now has an imprisonment rate of 149 per 100,000 of the population, compared with 100 in France and 77 In Germany. Black people continue to be over-represented in prisons (read *The New Jim Crow*, **Michelle Alexander**).

*"Rocketing prison numbers, a shocking surge in assaults and deaths by suicide in custody, fewer staff, less constructive activity and unacceptably high reconviction rates are the flashing warning lights that ministers must heed. To avert a crisis, they must check the bruising pace of change in the justice system and pay proper attention to ensuring that we*

*have decent, safe prisons. Over 40% of prisoners are now held in institutions of 1,000 places or more, and nearly two-thirds of prisons in England and Wales are overcrowded. An over-reliance on the use of imprisonment while slashing prison budgets and warehousing ever greater numbers overseen by fewer staff is no way to transform rehabilitation.* **Juliet Lyon,** Director of the Prison Reform Trust (www.prisonreformtrust.org.uk/PressPolicy/News/vw/1/ItemID/214)

The New Economics Foundation (NEF) and Centre for Justice Innovation are leading an ongoing investigation, *Beyond Crime and Punishment*. To read this report and get involved go to: www.neweconomics.org/projects/entry/better-courts www.neweconomics.org

**In contrast, the UK's five richest families are worth more than the poorest 20%.** In *A Tale of Two Britains: Inequality in the UK*, Oxfam reported that the UK's five wealthiest people are worth £28.2bn more than the whole of the bottom 20% of the population, and the gap between rich and poor continues to grow. In the UK, five billionaires have a combined wealth of £28.2bn, more than the bottom 20% 12.6 million people worth £28.1bn. The UK's 100 wealthiest people have as much money as the poorest 18 million – 30% of all households. The incomes of the UK's wealthiest 0.1% have grown nearly four times faster than the least well-off percentage of the population.

Oxfam says the findings are *"deeply worrying"*, and that such inequality is a *"sign of economic failure"*. Their report argues that widening inequality is creating a *"vicious circle where wealth and power are increasingly concentrated in the hands of a few, leaving the rest behind. This means the rules* are constantly rewritten in favour of the rich, for example, through policies such as lower taxes for high earners."

"Britain is becoming a deeply divided nation, with a wealthy elite who are seeing their incomes spiral up, whilst millions of families are struggling to make ends meet. It's deeply worrying that these extreme levels of wealth inequality exist in Britain today, where just a handful of people have more money than millions struggling to survive on the breadline."
**Ben Phillips,** Oxfam's Director of Campaigns and Policy

The Equality Trust, an independent think tank, estimated that the consequences of rising inequality cost the nation £39bn a year through its impact on health, wellbeing and crime rates. Then there is the loss to the economy of all those wasted resources.

A Labour spokesman said:

"While people on low and middle incomes are worse off, David Cameron has given the top 1% of earners a £3bn tax cut this year. He's totally out of touch with ordinary people and always stands up for the privileged few."

George Monbiot points out how taxation policies favour the very rich in his article, *Breaking the Silence, The Guardian*, 2nd December 2014 (www.monbiot.com/2014/12/02/breaking-the-silence). Sporting estates are exempt from business rates. David Cameron has almost doubled the public subsidy for English grouse moors and frozen the price of shotgun licenses at a public cost of £17m pa. Council tax banding and the payment of farm subsidies under which landowners are paid by the hectare both favour major owners of property. George Monbiot asks why capital gains tax (at 28%) is lower than the top rate of income tax; why principal residences, though their value may rise by millions, are altogether exempt; why rural landowners are typically excused of capital gains tax, inheritance tax, and the first five years of income tax. He notes that house prices have risen partly because the price of land has risen from 2% of the cost of a house in the 1930s to 70% today. He favours a Land Tax, as proposed in Chapter 7. He concludes:

*"For centuries, Britain has been a welfare state for patrimonial capital. It's time we broke it open, and broke the culture of deference that keeps us in our place. Let's bring the Highland Spring south, and start discussing some dangerous subjects."*

The Scottish government will soon have the opportunity to remedy some of these policies.

## *Conclusions*

Chris Mould, Chairman of the Trussell Trust, which provided 1,084,604 people with emergency food 1st April 2014 – 31st March 2015 (for 2011 to 2012, the figure was 128,697), is reported to have said:

*"It is not true to say that we have all been in this together. It is time we were honest about that and made the decision about whether we are happy with that."*

This is in the fifth or sixth richest economy in the world.

#### bruce nixon

The authors of the report, *Social Policy in a Cold Climate*, published November 2014, Paola De Agostini of Essex University of Essex and Professor John Hills at the LSE, say: *"The reforms had the effect of making an income transfer from the poorer half of households (and some of the very richest) to most of the richer half, with no net effect on the public finances."*

So far, from addressing the root causes of inequality and poverty, the Coalition appeared to have put most of its energy into what turned out to be punitive measures against the poor.

## *Taxation*

***Tax avoidance and evasion.*** To complete the picture, we need to include tax-havens. According to the Tax Justice Network's Financial Secrecy Index, $21-$32 trillion of private financial wealth is located, untaxed or lightly taxed, in secrecy jurisdictions around the world. The traditional stereotype of tax-havens is misconceived. The world's most important providers of financial secrecy are not small islands as many suppose, but some of the world's biggest and wealthiest countries. While the UK is ranked in 21st place on the index, it *"supports and partly controls"* a web of secrecy jurisdictions, marking it out as a leading offender. They say: *"The UK is the most important player in the financial secrecy world."* Then, of course, there are big corporations such as Pfizer, in the news as I write, who move their activities around the world in order to avoid taxation (Source: www.financialsecrecyindex.com/#intro).

Transparency International revealed how the purchase of more than 36,000 properties has been financed by offshore havens, all of which contributes to the vastly inflated London property market, which makes it harder and harder for Londoners to live in London. As they move out, property inflation spreads (www.transparency.org/news/pressrelease/uk_property_gives_global_corrupt_a_home). London has become a home for corrupt money (www.transparency.org/news/feature/property_in_the_uk_a_home_for_corrupt_money). Australia is cracking down on foreigners buying homes (www.bloomberg.com/news/articles/2015-02-25/australia-cracks-down-on-illegal-buying-of-homes-by-foreigners).

**Some taxes are regressive.** Regressive taxes are those paid by everyone at the same rate – rich and poor. So VAT, at 20%, increased from 17% by the Coalition, matters a lot more to ordinary working people than it does to the rich.

## Other ways in which citizens are robbed

**The great sell-off.** Once elected in 1979, Margaret Thatcher began a great sell-off of state assets that citizens had paid for. She introduced the Right to Buy for council house tenants to create a property-owning nation. But she did not build new, affordable homes to replace them. So we end up with a housing crisis, particularly affecting people on lower incomes. The housing crisis also has adverse consequences for employers. We now need to build affordable and sustainable housing with an ambition comparable to Clement Attlee's post-war house-building programme.

### bruce nixon

Margaret Thatcher started selling off publicly-owned companies to create greater efficiency and a nation of small shareholders. In fact, when she came to power, 40% of shares were owned by individuals; by the time she died, it was fewer than 12%. Gas, electricity and water companies were privatised and eventually British Rail. The irony is that state-owned, commercialised European rail firms now own more than a quarter of our rail system. And our rail fares are the highest in Europe; subsidies go down and train fares go up, like electricity, gas, water bills and director's salaries, far above inflation. The burden of paying for infrastructure improvements is shifted to the often-struggling users. Particularly in the provision of gas, electricity, water and sewerage, there is no effective competition when much of the market structure is an oligopoly, or as in the case of railways, hardly any competition is possible.

*"Not only are the privatised utilities big, remote corporations; most of them are no longer British, and no longer owned by small shareholders. Indeed, electricity and water privatisation could not have failed more absolutely to foster the emergence of world-beating, innovative British companies. Most of the electricity made and sold in England is now owned by dynamic, tech-savvy companies from Western Europe, a region doomed, Thatcher thought, by creeping socialism. As a direct result of the way electricity was privatised, much of it has now been renationalised – but by France, not Britain. Of the nine big English water and sewerage firms, six have achieved the seemingly impossible feat of being privatised a second time, delisted from the stock market by East Asian conglomerates or by private equity consortia. (Sale of the century: the privatisation scam,* **James Meek**, *author of Private Island: Why Britain Now Belongs to Someone Else*

### the 21st century revolution

– www.theguardian.com/politics/2014/aug/22/sale-of-century-privatisation-scam)

Importantly, there are alternative forms of ownership for key public services: public benefit companies with a founding charter, setting out its obligations to deliver public benefits.

***There is no evidence that privatisation necessarily works better than public ownership.*** The duty of the directors of a private company is to the shareholders, not the public or other stakeholders – for example, the six energy companies monopolising both supply and distribution. On the face of it, privatisation is likely to lead to higher costs as profit has to be added. What probably makes the most difference is the quality of leadership and management and whether or not there are conflicts of interest, as in the UK National Health Service.

Water Justice, part of the Economic Justice programme, a global organisation, studying numerous examples all over the world, found no empirical support for the argument that water privatisation necessarily leads to cost savings (www.tni.org/article/water-privatization-does-not-yield-cost-savings). Interestingly, East Coast trains in public ownership made a profit for the state and required the second lowest subsidy, "£19m compared with the highest, Northern Rail's £707.3m subsidy! (*Revealed – Britain's most subsidised routes* www.dailymail.co.uk/wires/pa/article-2730932/Figures-reveal-costs-commuters.html).

The London Olympic Games G4S security was a fiasco. The privatisation of public sector organisations

**bruce nixon**

such as Royal Mail, the shares being offered at knock-down prices, is another example of the taxpayer being robbed. Share values rapidly increased. Birmingham's local government and hospitals services being privatised, and the resulting inability to obtain information as the contracts are confidential. The Public Accounts Committee, Campaign4Change, BBC Radio 4's *File on Four*, *Analysis* and *Keep our NHS Public* are exposing the stealth privatisation and the high costs and profits, secrecy and failures that often result.

Despite these lessons, privatisation is spreading into the NHS, local government, security services, state schools, and the prison and probation services. Surely services so important to the nation, such as these, should not be in the hands of the private sector.

A further important insight is that when consumers have no option but to buy services that are essential to life, they are in effect paying a tax when they are over-charged. Will Hutton describes rail fares, the highest in Europe going higher, as *"a poll tax on wheels"* ([www.theguardian.com/profile/willhutton+commentisfree/commentisfree](www.theguardian.com/profile/willhutton+commentisfree/commentisfree)).

*"If a payment to an authority, public or private, is compulsory, it's a tax. We can't do without electricity; the electricity bill is an electricity tax. We can't do without water; the water bill is a water tax. Some people can get by without railways, and some can't; they pay the rail tax. Students pay the university tax. The meta-privatisation is the privatisation of the tax system itself; even, it could be said, the privatisation of us, the former citizens of Britain. By packaging British citizens up and selling them, sector by sector, to investors,*

### the 21st century revolution

*the Government makes it possible to keep traditional taxes low or even cut them. By moving from a system where public services are supported by progressive general taxation to a system where they are supported exclusively by the flat fees people pay to use them, they move from a system where the rich are obliged to help the poor to a system where the less well-off enable services that the rich get for what is, to them, a trifling sum."*

Another example was when Royal Mail was sold off too cheaply; again, we were robbed.

The latest sell-off is the UK's 40% stake in Eurostar for £750m. But was this wise?

Cumulatively, private sales abroad over the past 10 years amount to £440bn. Many of our great public or private companies built by visionary entrepreneurs and committed employees have been sold or bought by speculators or private equity firms through highly leveraged deals. Many such deals do not benefit the nation or the company; they burden the company with debt, lead to job losses, and adversely affect the interests of employees, including their pensions, and the local community. When ownership passes out of Britain, strategic decisions are made elsewhere; national interests are no longer taken into account. Often, research associated with our top universities moves out of our country. We end up losing key industries and skills, and a weakened economy with all the social consequences. Such policies need to be rethought.

A prime example is Boots. In June 2007, the American venture capital firm, KKR, pulled off Europe's largest private equity deal. With an Italian entrepreneur, KKR bought the company for £11.1bn by borrowing £9.3bn. It was the first private equity takeover of a FTSE 100 firm. The deal created an enormous burden of debt. Boots' headquarters moved from Nottingham to the Swiss tax-haven canton of Zug. The UK lost out in taxes; about 900 jobs were lost, many from the Nottingham HQ. In the preceding year, Alliance Boots plc made profits of around £455m and paid £131m tax. Boots had been a profitable, tax-paying, British company for over 150 years. Boots generally paid about one-third of its profits in UK tax, and HM Revenue could expect about £150m each year. By the March 2008 accounts, it made a pre-tax loss of £64m and reported a tax credit of £74m in 2008. Since then, it has avoided £1bn in tax. However, as a result of War on Want campaigners, Alliance Boots, who draw an estimated 40% of its UK revenues – £4 billion from prescriptions and related services – mainly paid for by the UK's taxpayer-funded National Health Service, are now being forced to pay more tax (War on Want www.waronwant.org/resources/alliance-boots-tax-gap).

Our European friends, like Germany and France, are wiser.

**Private Finance Initiatives and (PFI) Public Private Partnerships (PPPs)** are ways of funding public infrastructure projects with private capital. They are devices used to avoid debt appearing on the Government's books. These have been used to pay for new hospitals or schools but have often proved far more expensive than if the taxpayer had funded such investments, and the hospital or school has got into financial difficulties as a result. Moreover, Margaret Hodge, Chair of the Commons Public Accounts Committee, has revealed how companies earn

## the 21st century revolution

hundreds of millions by *"selling on"* 25-year contracts for hospitals and schools. It is reported that four contractors alone made profits of more than £300m. Of the companies studied – Balfour Beatty, Carillion, Interserve and Kier – Balfour Beatty is by far the biggest beneficiary of the rising value of its Private Finance Initiative and Public Private Partnership deals. It alone has made profits of £188.9m (www.independent.co.uk/news/uk/politics/exclusive-how-private-firms-make-quick-killing-from-pfi-9488351.html).

**Other rackets.** We ordinary taxpayers subsidise businesses that don't pay a living wage through tax credits and we pay the bill for the social and health costs of the poverty to which they have contributed. Then there is the enormous loss caused by the undeveloped talents of our people. The housing crisis, caused by insufficient building of affordable homes for decades and the use of property as an investment, is causing the housing benefits bill to soar. As a result, we are subsidising landlords whose residents can't afford the rent. We subsidise big companies who massively avoid tax, yet benefit from the public infrastructure and services that we have paid for and continue to do so. Why do we let them get away with it, with the connivance of Government? However, we exploit all those people in poor countries, some of them slaves, working for little money, sometimes in appalling conditions, producing cheap food and clothing that does not last. Amongst the worst consequences for us of this drive to the bottom is the loss of good work in our country, large-scale unemployment, insecurity, ill health and loss of wellbeing. Again, we end up paying the social costs. On top of that, we have to keep buying more stuff because things don't last and rapidly become obsolete. Does any of this make sense?

**Theft by the rich.** The stories above, and earlier, about how citizens saved the reckless bankers, illustrate how the ordinary citizen is the victim of theft on a grand scale. Theft by ordinary criminals is nothing in comparison to the theft by the rich. They are colonising poor countries and now they are colonising us! No wonder living standards and conditions of employment of the majority and the poorest in our society have been steadily declining for a generation and young people are so worried about their prospects.

## *The role of the state*

*"The important thing for Government is not to do things which individuals are doing already, and to do them a little better or a little worse; but to do those things which at present are not done at all."* **John Maynard Keynes**

It is essential the state is clear about what it's for. A government under the influence of Neoliberalism is likely to have a lack of clarity about the respective roles of the state and private sectors.

**The Roles of the Public and Private Sectors.** Simply put, the public sector is there to ensure that the long-term needs of the country are met, essential public services are provided, and there is a safety net for the less fortunate in society, which can affect all of us. A prime example is health, where professional values and motivation are in danger of being compromised by financial interests, as in the case of GPs, instead of all stakeholders, now being given responsibility for sourcing. Education and fundamental scientific research should remain in the public sector as it is there to serve the nation as a whole, not distorted by the interests of business. Also, as we have seen, the private sector is not necessarily more efficient or cost-effective than the public sector, e.g. in the management of prisons and the probation service, and G4S' bungled Olympics security contract that had to be bailed out by troops, and the high cost of rail travel and energy.

The state should be there to do what business is unlikely to do, such as providing long-term support for research and development into the new industries of the future. That is what the most successful economies have done and are doing, including the USA and the growing economies, BRICS and South East Asia. Another example is the provision of affordable housing in sufficiently large numbers, which developers cannot risk doing because of the vicissitudes of the market. This is partly why the plans to force housing associations to release their housing on a Right to Buy is so flawed.

Too much influenced by the Neoliberal ideology and the "tyranny" of the Treasury, the UK's Coalition Government appeared confused about the respective roles of private and public sectors. Nor did they recognise the importance of trade unions as a counterbalance to the power of big business (we get the unions we deserve). Relying on the market plainly does not work. The Coalition, like New Labour before them, privatised health, care services, education, public research and other public services, and all of which should be independent of big business that is obliged to put the interests of shareholders first. The state is there to protect its citizens from the abuses and excesses of power. The Coalition believed in minimising regulation. Of course, regulation should be limited to what is essential; otherwise, it becomes a burden on legitimate enterprise. A balance needs to be achieved. This will continue under the new Tory government unless there is sufficient opposition.

**Market Failure and Regulatory Capture.** The role of governments – the occasions that business cannot undertake the activity properly – are (1) when the project is too big/complex (2) too risky (3) payoff is too far in the future. There are certain activities that are intermediate goods that form the bedrock of the rest of the economy – transport, utilities, education, health, etc. These really are natural monopolies that act as inputs to the rest of the economy. So when private firms undertake them, the likelihood of exploitation is high. This is demonstrated by their response to regulation. The Office of Gas and Electricity Markets (OFGEM), The Water Services Regulation Authority (OFWAT), The Groceries Code Adjudicator (or Supermarket Ombudsman) and similar organisations have thus far proved too weak. Regulatory capture was a factor in the financial crisis. The Financial Services Authority was inadequate in the face of industry lobbying and the revolving door, and has now been replaced by two new agencies (the Prudential Regulation Authority and the Financial Conduct Authority) and the Bank of England.

Yvonne Roberts sums up the result of these policies:

*"The number of children living in poverty is growing enormously. The terrible irony of the last three decades, under Labour, the Conservatives and the Coalition, is that the effort to minimalize regulation, weaken trade unions and*

## the 21st century revolution

*liberalise the financial markets has patently failed to propel modern capitalism to greater heights. On the contrary, when even the International Monetary Fund disputes right-wing politicians who claim inequality is an incentive to the rich to make more and a spur to the poor to work harder, the project is in deep trouble.*

*Since 2003, economic growth has decoupled from earnings. According to the Office for National Statistics (ONS), output per man-hour in the UK is 21 percentage points below the G7 average, the biggest productivity gap since 1992. Britain is 30 percentage points less productive than Germany, France and the United States. We are becoming a low-productivity, low-wage economy, with desperately poor exports. Our 'flexible' workforce is enabled by underemployment that wastes talents, while a lack of training bodes ill for the future."*

Meanwhile, according to the Institute for Fiscal Studies:

*"Unless there is change, the number of children in poverty in one of the most affluent countries in the world will grow by an additional 400,000 over the course of this Parliament. This is not only appalling in its own right; it is detrimental to society and the economy."* (www.theguardian.com/commentisfree/2014/aug/10/britain-state-failing-need-for-new-modern-state-ethos)

Professor Mariana Mazzucato, author of *The Entrepreneurial State: Debunking Private vs Public Sector Myths* (www.theguardian.com/commentisfree/2014/jul/20/public-banks-brics-countries-financial-markets), argues that an important role of government is not only to kick-start recovery through wise spending but (as has been proved in the most successful economies) to provide finance for innovation, which requires patient, long-term, committed finance. This is what the BRICS – Brazil, Russia, India, China and South Africa – are doing in setting up a $50bn new development bank with a $100bn contingent reserve arrangement. These were the sort of sensible arrangements set up at the end of WW2 with Keynes' advice. She points out that venture capital, which was meant to be more risk-loving than private banks, has become short-termist, focused on early exits, when innovation can take up to 15-20 years. Public banks need to be lead investors in funding the next technological revolution, including green innovation. This is how the internet and biotech were funded.

It is now apparent that the banks were not serving the real economy but recklessly funding finance and making irresponsible loans. The necessary radical reforms have still not been made.

## *Growing unrest*

As discussed in the first chapter, politics today is too much about the tactics of gaining power and holding on to it, rather than working with everyone to create a long-term vision and bring it about. Paul Hawken spoke of *Blessed Unrest* in his book of that name; *"Non-violent unrest will ultimately transform this rotten, dangerous system."* (www.blessedunrest.com)

To succeed in rising to the unprecedented challenges we face, we need a fully-functioning, modern democracy. That depends on having well-informed citizens and high-quality

## the 21st century revolution

media available to everyone that people can trust. The good news is that most young people use the internet for information and dialogue – not the old 20th century media. They lobby from there. Amongst the biggest obstacles to change are our corrupt democracy with its antiquated rituals and the power we give to the super rich and big business, *"the ruling class"*, as George Orwell described them, and our widespread feelings of indifference and powerlessness.

The underlying issues have not much changed since George Orwell said in **Why I Write**:

*"England is the most class-ridden country under the sun. It is a land of snobbery and privilege, ruled largely by the old and silly."*

How much have things changed? Perhaps now it is not just the *old and silly*. Certainly, this fits the decisions to go to war.

**Chumocracy.** The public also see a self-serving political class, too many with privileged backgrounds and little experience of the *"real"* world of working life. There are too many Etonians in high office.

**Sexism.** Sound decisions about our nation's wellbeing cannot be made when women are not equally represented in Parliament. The lack of women in political positions of power is a real democratic deficit. Part of the problem is that Parliament is not women-friendly. They complain of widespread sexism and being excluded from important discussions.

### bruce nixon

**The good news is that many are campaigning to get more women into Parliament.** For example, the Counting Women In campaign is aiming for 50/50 gender representation at all levels of national, local and devolved government (www.countingwomenin.org/index.php/counting-women-in), and the 50:50 Parliament (www.5050parliament.co.uk). Another organisation promoting women as leaders in all walks of life is UN Women (www.unwomen.org/en/about-us/about-un-women).

Apart from the injustice of discrimination, we cannot afford to exclude women from any aspect in society. Nations that remove the obstacles to women engaging at the highest levels of the arts, science, medicine and engineering, to take a few examples, flourish far more than those that don't. Women science professors in the UK on average are paid £5,000 less than men; in some universities, the difference can be as much as £21,000. In a world where scientific innovation is so important for national prosperity, discrimination of this kind is so damaging.

Nicola Sturgeon, Scotland's First Minister, says:

*"Being the first woman First Minister is a big responsibility and I feel the weight of that acutely. I'm determined to use that position to help further the ability of other women to get on in their chosen field... Quotas are necessary. They're a blunt tool. But if we had a real meritocracy now, we'd have a gender balance. I appointed a gender-balanced cabinet – one of only three in the developed world. I'm challenging companies and public bodies to have gender balance on their boards. I'm extending childcare to give women practical help to pursue careers. If I leave office... without*

### the 21st century revolution

*having helped make a difference for other women then that would be a failure.* (Thanks to **Oliver Duff**, Thursday 12th February 2015 – www.independent.co.uk/news/uk/politics/generalelection/nicola-sturgeon-i-want-to-help-women-10042980.html)

The narrative has been negative when a positive one was needed. That silly phrase, *"hard-working people"*, trotted out by out-of-touch *"toffs"* is patronising. Their ideology is justified by *"lazy stereotypes, divisive discourse and misleading statistics"*. (*Towards a New Social Settlement*, New Economics Foundation (NEF) –www.neweconomics.org/blog/entry/towards-a-new-social-settlement) Of course, there are some scroungers, but the focus should be on the much more damaging super-rich scroungers, getting to the root of the problem and creating a healthy economy that provides opportunity.

**Who are the real scroungers?** Surely they are the irresponsible bankers who got us in this mess, ripped us off, still pay themselves disproportionate salaries and bonuses, and get bailed out by the taxpayers. Surely it is the employers who pay their employees so little that their wages have to be supplemented by us taxpayers; and the companies and business leaders who avoid and evade paying taxes, and the MPs who fiddle their expenses and get paid by companies for lobbying. And the big corporations like oil companies and airlines, often subsidised by us, who are making profits at the expense of consumers and driving humanity to the brink of disaster. In his article, *Cut benefits? Yes, let's start with our £85bn corporate welfare hand-out*, Aditya Chakrabortty exposed the huge, hidden hand-outs to corporations, many of whom also avoid vast sums (www.

**bruce nixon**

theguardian.com/commentisfree/2014/oct/06/benefits-corporate-welfare-research-public-money-businesses). These are the real big-time scroungers and skivers, not Ian Duncan Smith's targets.

It is an outrage. Yet, over the centuries, we British have been conditioned not to feel our rage in case there would be an insurrection.

***Young people are generally disengaged from politics and the media.*** If they are engaged, their access to information and activism is the internet, not the traditional media. Up to 800,000 young Britons were not on the voters' register (Electoral Reform Society www.electoral-reform.org.uk). Their first concern is to establish a rewarding way of earning a good living and ultimately buying a home. And, of course, having a good time and being what it is to be young. Many young people are seeking work or those in work well below their capability. Often they are saddled with a burden of debt because the Government is not prepared to pay the cost of the nation's education.

According to the Sutton Trust, most students will still be paying back loans from their university days in their 40s and 50s, and many will never clear the debt.

*"We estimate that students will leave university with nearly £20,000 more debt, on average, in 2014 prices (£44,035 under the new system, compared with £24,754 under the old system). The vast majority of this increase is the result of higher fee loans to cover higher tuition fees."*

## the 21st century revolution

In cash terms, graduates will now repay a total of £66,897 on average – equating to £35,446 in 2014 prices.

Germany supports many more students than in the UK without charging tuition fees, and welcomes international students.

Throughout Europe, there are large numbers of underemployed or unemployed young people. They have no confidence in the ability of politicians to change things for the better.

**Feeling powerless is just what suits the "ruling class"**, as George Orwell described them.

Too much of the daily news is bad news. Good news rarely makes the headlines. People are in dire need of hope.

"People in debt become hopeless and hopeless people don't vote," **Tony Benn** once said.

"Getting depressed about the situation now is like sitting inert in your living room and watching the kitchen catch fire, and then getting more and more miserable as the fire spreads throughout the house – rather than grabbing an extinguisher and dousing the flames." **Mark Lynas**, author of **Six Degrees – our future on a hotter planet**.

**Illiterate political leaders.** Amongst the biggest obstacles to progress are economically, environmentally and ecologically illiterate political leaders, and a confused public believing there is nothing they can do.

**bruce nixon**

All this can be changed.

## *Conclusion*

***We are at a great turning point.*** All over the world, there are large numbers of independent think and act tanks and powerful lobbying organisations, some involving millions of people. There is a growing consensus about the situation we are in and what needs to be done. There is no shortage of well-researched, radical policies and fresh ideas to tackle all our environmental, economic and social problems. A fair society works best. These are the sources of new values and a change of consciousness. This is where the energy and leadership for benign change will come from.

Recently, I went to the Compass Conference in London, *Change How 2015*. It was one of the most inspiring events I have ever been to. 520 people came, many of whom were young. There were a hundred speakers to choose from, operating in seven rooms, speaking for fifteen minutes, each offering lots of fresh ideas, proposals, stories and campaigns (www.change-how.com). On the following weekend, I attended the Global Justice Now conference, *Take back our world!*, attended by some 730 people (www.globaljustice.org.uk). In both cases, I went away refreshed and inspired. The Transition Town Network, a powerful global movement for bringing about progressive change in communities all over the world, is spreading – see Resources at the end of the book.

### the 21st century revolution

***Human beings have struggled with the same fundamental issues throughout history.*** Environmental crises are not new. Exploitation of the Earth has been the undoing of many previous civilisations. On the one hand, there is greed, desire for power and privilege, and intolerance of difference. It has led to injustice, exploitation, cruelty, genocide, violence and war. On the other, there have always been progressive forces; people who want a better, fairer world in which there is justice – everyone has the chance of a fulfilled life and difference is valued. There have always been the forces of resistance, people who resist change that threatens their perceived interests – the wealthy, big business, financiers and political parties representing them. When William Morris was writing and speaking about these issues at the end of the 19th century, he was far ahead of his time. His book, *News from Nowhere*, offered a Utopian dream, very similar to what we might support today. But he had little or no idea about how to bring it about. Today we do.

The big difference today is that these issues are on a global scale; we are at war with Mother Earth and we will lose – unless we choose to act decisively.

***Just one person can make a big difference.*** Neil Jameson, one of the founders of Citizens UK, led a march in London to launch the Living Wage campaign in 2010 (www.livingwage.org.uk). On 1st November 2014, it was reported that over 1,000 companies were committed to paying the living wage or above, securing tens of millions of pounds in extra pay for the working poor. The current living wage is £8.80 in London and £7.65 elsewhere. In 2013, 432 companies were accredited by the Living Wage

Foundation, a part of community organisation, **Citizens UK** (www.citizensuk.org). That figure has now more than doubled, as hundreds of other organisations, charities and businesses have signed up. And, importantly, Neil Jameson gained cross-party support. The surge in numbers, and the burgeoning campaign to lift the pay of the worst-off, means that about 60,000 people will get a pay rise. The living wage differs from the national minimum wage, currently £6.50 per hour for those aged over 21. There are similar campaigns in the USA and Canada.

# Chapter 3

## The environmental challenge – we're sleepwalking to disaster

*"Anyone who believes exponential growth can go on forever in a finite world is either a madman or an economist."*
**Kenneth Boulding**

**Our survival is threatened** by climate change, extreme weather and the destruction of the ecological system on which all life depends. It is not just *"peak-oil"* that made our extraordinary way of life possible in the 20th century; it is *"peak-everything"*. We now consume 30% more than Planet Earth can sustain and our appetite is growing. We have been warned many times by scientists and economists such as Lord Stern. The longer we delay in taking responsible action, the worse it will get and the more it will cost. This has been amply demonstrated by the winter floods and coastal storms in England, and the appalling floods and loss of life in South East Asia.

Sir David King, UK's Special Representative for Climate Change, leading the UK's efforts to secure an ambitious deal at the UN Climate Change Conference in Paris in December 2015, says, *"Progress has been painfully close to zero,"* And, in 2015, *"... more critical to the future of our civilization than 1945"*, when the UN was created following two world wars. Climate change, he said, is the *"biggest threat facing mankind at this moment"* (International Business Times, 11th June 2015).

We urgently need to slow and reverse climate change before it is too late. We also need measures of adaption and mitigation. The situation will become out of control if we leave it too long – some say we now have 33 months before we reach a tipping point (One Hundred Months – www.onehundredmonths.org).

***A very dangerous experiment.*** The Report of Intergovernmental Panel Climate Change (IPCC), September 2013 – the work of some 2,000 scientists all over the world – said, with 95% certainty, that humans are the dominant cause of global warming since the 1950s. Professor Sir Brian Hoskins, Imperial College London, told BBC News:

*"We are performing a very dangerous experiment with our planet, and I don't want my grandchildren to suffer the consequences of that experiment."*

The 15th April 2014 IPCC update warns:

*"Only major institutional and technological change will give a better than even chance that global warming will not exceed 2°C by the end of the century, an internationally agreed-upon threshold. The report makes clear that if we're going to avoid catastrophic climate change, we need to get out of investing in fossil fuels."* **Oscar Reyes** (www.trust.org/item/20140415135531-yfzg4)

## the 21st century revolution

An earlier update, published on 31$^{st}$ March 2014, warned that the impacts will vary widely from country to country, with poorer countries bearing the brunt. Food security is highlighted as an area of significant concern. Crop yields for maize, rice and wheat will all be hit in the period up to 2050, with around a tenth of projections showing losses over 25%. After 2050, the risk of more severe yield impacts increases. Demand for food from a population estimated to be around nine billion will rise.

Michel Jarraud, Secretary-General of the World Meteorological Organization, said that, previously, people could have damaged the Earth's climate out of *"ignorance"*. He said:

*"Now, ignorance is no longer a good excuse."*

Jim Yong Kim, 12$^{th}$ President of the World Bank, at the Opening Press Conference of the World Bank/IMF Spring Meetings 2015, called for a carbon tax and immediate scrapping of all subsidies for fossil fuels. At the forthcoming UN talks in Paris, he wanted to see a binding international agreement to a zero-carbon world by 2100, and $100bn finance to help poor countries adapt to climate change.

One thing we can be sure of is that we need to persuade the world to leave oil, coal and gas reserves worth many trillions of dollars in the ground (*The Burning Question* www.burningquestion.info). There will be enormous health benefits if we do so. For example, air pollution causes 29,000 early deaths a year in the UK – more than obesity and alcohol combined (Client Earth – www.clientearth.org). In the USA, the corresponding figure is 200,000. The global figure was seven million in 2012. I shall come back to this later in this chapter.

**However, it is essential to see these warnings in a positive light**. These challenges present enormous opportunities for the peoples of all nations to work together to create a better way of life for everyone. Instead of competing, we need to work together to empower ourselves and use our collective creativity. The message is *"collaborate or perish"*. I think the universe, nature, is trying to teach us a lesson. We have to live more lightly on our planet. It is natural to love each other and Mother Nature. More and more stuff does not make us happier; and it makes many others very unhappy. All we need is enough.

## *Global warming*

*"The impacts of global warming are likely to be severe, pervasive and irreversible."* **Intergovernmental Panel on Climate Change (IPCC)**, second report 2014

Can any warning be stronger? The warming climate will place the world under enormous strain, forcing mass migration, especially in Asia, and increasing the risk of violent conflict. There are also major health risks. Climate change will reduce median crop yields by 2% per decade for the rest of the century – at a time of rapidly-growing demand. This will push up malnutrition in children by about a fifth, it predicts. The report also forecasts that the warming climate will take its toll on human health, pushing up the number of intense heatwaves and fires, and increasing the risk from food and water-borne diseases.

## the 21st century revolution

Biofuel production will add to food shortage and is not a sustainable solution.

***Global greenhouse gas (GHG) emissions have grown since pre-industrial times***, with an increase of 70% between 1970 and 2004. Since 1950, the Earth has warmed by 0.7°C due to greenhouse gas emissions, deforestation and other human activities. Temperatures are likely rise a further 0.3°C to 0.7°C in the period 2016-2035. The world is likely to be 0.4° warmer by the end of the century unless we act. Seasons have shifted by about seven days since 1990. In its report, released on September 27th, 2013, the IPCC estimated sea levels could rise 28 to 98 cm (a maximum of more than three feet) by 2100 — more than 50% higher than 2007 projections (Yale Environment 360. 21 Oct 2013).

While, initially, the impact on the UK will be comparatively small, global issues such as rising food prices are already posing serious problems, especially for people on modest or very low incomes – a growing proportion of UK citizens. Britain's health and environmental cultural heritage is also likely to be hurt. The UK's already elevated air pollution is likely to worsen as burning fossil fuels increase ozone levels, while warmer weather will increase the incidence of asthma and hay fever (Source: Tom Bawden, *The Independent*, Tuesday 18th March 2014).

***Air Pollution.*** Worldwide every year around 7 million people and 400,000 in Europe are dying prematurely as a result of air pollution.

It is such an important omission. The World Health Organization (WHO) now classifies diesel exhaust as a cause of cancer. While advances in technology have helped clean up diesel pollution, the findings have serious implications for developing countries still relying on dirty diesel power (*World Health Organization Says Diesel Exhaust Causes Cancer* – www.cancer.org/cancer/news/world-health-organization-says-diesel-exhaust-causes-cancer).

Recent high levels of air pollution in the UK have drawn attention to the contribution of exhaust fumes in causing cancer, especially those from the growing use of diesel engines in cars (now 51% of sales are diesel). Diesel engine emissions are said to pose the single greatest public health challenge for UK cities in the years to come (*Particulate air pollution: health effects of exposure* – www.gov.uk/government/publications/particulate-air-pollution-health-effects-of-exposure).

Considerable improvements in diesel engines have been made but it will take time for the older vehicles to be replaced. If we choose to walk and cycle instead of driving, there will be even greater health benefits, fewer deaths and severe injuries on our roads, plus enormous savings for our struggling NHS (*The Energy Glut* by Professor Ian Roberts – www.roadpeace.org/involved/support_us/the_energy_glut). Something like half its budget could be saved.

***An ultra-low emission zone in London from 2020*** is good news. London faces massive fines from the EU, particularly due to nitrous oxide from diesel. The EU says that levels of nitrogen dioxide, mainly from diesel engines, are excessive in many British cities. Transport for London (TfL) has completed its public consultation on plans to

## the 21st century revolution

create the *"world's first"* ultra-low emission zone (ULEZ) in a capital from 2020. It encompasses the Central London area, based on the congestion charge map. The zone will *"significantly improve air quality and the health of Londoners"* by reducing the number of areas where nitrogen dioxide (NO2) levels currently exceed legal limits by 74% in Central London, 51% in inner London, and 43% in outer London. Cars, motorcycles, vans, minibuses, heavy goods vehicles and coaches will have to meet new standards or pay a daily charge to drive in the zone. Taxis, private hire vehicles and buses would also be affected.

From 1st January 2018, all newly licensed taxis – and new Private Hire Vehicles (PHVs) – must be Zero Emission Capable (ZEC). A £65m fund will encourage the take-up of new vehicles, making the capital's taxi fleet the cleanest and greenest in the world. The fund will help drivers upgrade to zero emission-capable taxis and "decommission" the oldest vehicles from the fleet. A 15-year age limit for taxis will encourage retirement of the oldest, most polluting taxis through a voluntary decommissioning scheme. From 2017, drivers of taxis over 10 years old will be able to claim up to £5,000, the precise amount depending on the age of their vehicle.

The intention is to give motorists adequate time to switch to greener vehicles. Introducing the Zone will *"accelerate the take-up of low emission vehicles and stimulate the low emission vehicle market"*. TfL says the majority of traffic entering the ULEZ will be from outside the zone, so the benefits of cleaner, greener vehicles will benefit Londoners' health right across London.

**bruce nixon**

If you want ULEZ to be introduced sooner, over a wider area and throughout all cities and towns in the UK, go to www.airqualitynews.com.

***Worldwide, in 2013, there were 41 weather disasters***, almost all of which involved water – flooding, drought or damage from cyclones. Drought is made worse by population growth. The USA experienced extreme snow; Australia had its hottest year on record, causing numerous bush fires. A tropical cyclone killed 5,700 people in the Philippines. Millions of people are at risk from severe drought, starvation and disease, and up to one-third of land-based species face extinction by the middle of the century (www.cat.org.uk/index.html).

In the UK, the 2013 winter was the wettest since records began in 1760, causing devastating floods in the Somerset Levels and beside the Thames, and severe coastal damage. In February 2014, the Thames Barrier was closed a record 28 times, bringing the winter total to 50. Over 25% of all flood defence closures since the Thames Barrier became operational in 1982 have been during the winter of 2013/14. These floods came after the worst droughts in 100 years.

The Thames Barrier has been raised 174 times since it became operational in 1982. Closures have steadily increased. Over three-quarters of closures have been since 2000. It was closed four times in the 1980s, 35 times in the 1990s, and 135 times since 2000. In winter, the 2013/14 total was 50. Over 25% of all flood defence closures since the Thames Barrier became operational in 1982 were during the 2013/14 winter. To reduce the chance of it failing to unacceptable levels, 50 closures a year is the maximum to ensure proper maintenance. If this continues, the Thames tidal defence system will need to be improved (London State of the Environment Report, 7th March 2014).

For everyone's sake, I hope the extreme weather events in the UK and all over the world in 2013/14 will be a wake-up call. We need to do everything we can to put pressure on our governments to agree and implement decisive action at the forthcoming International Climate Conference, COP 21, 21st Conference of the Parties on Climate Change 2015 in Paris, 30th November to 11th December 2015. The UN Conference in New York, 23rd September 2014, produced little commitment to action. Only $2.3bn was pledged for a Green Climate Fund **to help adapt** to climate change, note, **not prevent**. To put this into perspective, $11tn is spent by the gas and oil industries on developing new sources of hydrocarbons that should be left in the ground. India and Australia did not attend.

## *Ecocide*

We are also committing ecocide (defined as extensive damage to, destruction or loss of ecosystems – eradicatingecocide.com):
- Canada's Alberta Tar Sands produce four times more greenhouse gas emissions than conventional oil extraction, and uses enough natural gas to heat three million Canadian homes
- We are also damaging the lives of native people by such activities, and displacing them

- Pacific Trash Vortex – 100 million tonnes of floating rubbish, polluting the sea and coastlines
- 100 species become extinct every day
- Amazon forest: an area equal to 50 football pitches has been destroyed every minute since 2000. The total loss is 10 times the area of the UK (guardian.com, Friday 15th November)

We know ecocide is happening; yet, we prefer to not think about the consequences.

It cannot be said that the UK government was not warned. Yet they have done worse than next to nothing. Their half-hearted and inconsistent record is a major obstacle to exploiting the economic benefits of developing renewable energy, without resource to nuclear power, and boosting a growing industry providing exports and employment. George Osborne's *"We're not going to save the planet by putting our country out of business,"* is folly. As Chris Huhne said, *"We are not going to save our economy by turning our back on renewable energy."* We have been warned repeatedly that, the longer we delay, the higher the costs of Climate Chaos will be. And of course there will be no economy if we delay too long.

***Courageous and consistent leadership is needed.*** David Cameron declared the Coalition would be the *"Greenest government ever"*. Yet he appointed Owen Paterson, a well-known "denier", to the crucial role of Secretary of State for Environment. Then he decided to make cuts to the Energy Companies Obligation (ECO) that required energy companies to insulate homes and subsidise

## the 21st century revolution

energy efficiency measures for hard-to-treat properties. George Osborne said carbon-cutting measures will not be at the expense of British business. The Confederation of British Industry (CBI) said companies are serious about climate change but politicians are failing to provide certainty for investors. These inconsistencies have a very detrimental effect and they continue.

***Measures to retrofit Britain's millions of leaky buildings should be a top priority.*** We have a legal commitment to a 34% reduction in our greenhouse gas emissions by 2020 and a reduction of at least 80% by 2050 against 1990 levels. Buildings are a major contributor; over 40% of man-made emissions come from energy used in our homes and when we travel. 38% of the UK's total greenhouse gas emissions come from leaky buildings. Retrofitting the UK's leaky 25 million homes would mean *"3,000 homes to be kitted out every day for the next 37 years"*. It is an enormous task. However, not only would it lead to a considerable reduction in energy waste, it would help poorer people suffering cold and provide large numbers of jobs.

Yet, in December 2013, the Government cancelled the Green Levy on energy bills, resulting in severe cuts to Green scheme measures to help people make their homes warmer and more energy efficient. 2.26m homes that would have got help by 2017 were reduced to 1.82m. It also cut a lot of green jobs.

***Renewable Energy.*** Recently it was reported that the UK government, without consulting the Scottish government, whose plans are extensive, will remove subsidies from land-based wind farms, undermining that industry and putting many jobs at risk. These would generate 7.1 gigawatts, equivalent to about seven average-sized nuclear power reactors. At the same time, incentives are provided for fracking and local councils will be stripped of their power to decide on fracking proposals. The Centre for Alternative Technology's journal, *Clean Slate*, winter 2014, reported that G7 countries spend annually at least $8bn on direct subsidies and tax breaks for exploration of oil, gas and coal reserves, of which the UK contributes up to $1.2bn.

***Energy Bill Revolution.*** A campaign well worth supporting is the Energy Bill Revolution. They are calling for:

1. Home energy efficiency to be made a UK national infrastructure priority.
2. Two million UK low-income homes given grants to make their homes highly energy efficient (EPC Band C) by 2020, with all six million homes brought up to this standard by 2025.
3. Carbon tax revenue used to provide long-term funding for the programme.
4. 0% loans for energy efficiency measures for the able to pay.

This programme would create the world's most ambitious home energy efficiency programme, slashing energy bills and carbon emissions, creating over 100,000 jobs and helping end the fuel poverty crisis once and for all (www.energybillrevolution.org/whats-the-campaign/).

### the 21st century revolution

# The leadership issue again

*"Almost all our would-be leaders and their hangers-on are arguing about possible short-term political policies and alliances, while virtually none are interested in the one big question we face: how to avoid our potential suicide and achieve the survival of human civilisation."* **James Robertson** – Working for a sane alternative

Given that this is the prevailing mind-set of most political leaders, it is hardly surprising that the environment was at the bottom of citizens' list of 12 most important issues facing Britain (survey carried out by Opinion Research just before the General Election). In the UK's 2015 General Election campaign, with the exception of the Green Party, the environmental crisis was barely mentioned by the political leaders. At this time in human history, more than ever before, we need to promote the concept of stewardship leadership.

***I am reminded of the situation leading up to WW2***, as I said in the introduction. Appeasement was the name of the game until, finally, in 1940, Churchill formed a National Government, with Clement Attlee ultimately serving as Deputy Prime Minister. The UK rapidly transformed its economy to support the war effort. Within weeks of Pearl Harbor, USA declared war and did the same. Car production virtually ceased (only 139 more cars were made in USA during the entire war), and factories converted rapidly to producing aircraft. Production of Liberty Ships replaced the entire losses of allied lost ship tonnage since 1939. This demonstrates what we can do, given the decisive strategic leadership. Clement Attlee, a modest statesman, arguably the greatest British Prime Minister of the 20$^{th}$ century, knew how to lead, and led great men. How many younger people have even heard of him? (*Attlee: A Life in Politics* by Nicklaus Thomas-Symonds)

I quote from an e-mail to me from Nicklaus:

*"Great individuals are rarely seen as great at the time. Attlee was very understated, and did not see the Prime Minister as a facilitator of policy; rather, he had to ensure consensus was reached in Cabinet. Attlee's skill lay in getting the best out of a team of great men. He ensured their quarrelling did not undermine the Government. His 'chairmanship' model was very effective. The 1945 General Election manifesto, 'Let Us Face the Future', also gave the Government a clear sense of direction and purpose, together with achievable immediate goals. For me, the key is to have* **both vision and a set of practical policies** (my bold type)."

If only we had that quality of leadership now!

There are lessons here for what we need to do today to address an even more serious threat. Amongst these are: prevention is better than cure and costs less; we can rapidly mobilise and transform our economy if we decide to do so. A sense of urgency, leadership and will are lacking. To many of the public, the preoccupations of main party leaders in the run-up to the General Election seemed tactical, rather than farsighted and visionary.

There is another lesson. There is no sign of a 21$^{st}$ century Clement Attlee yet. So what do we do? We citizens have to provide the leadership; all of us, by every possible non-violent means, need to demand that the Government acts. If enough of us take our power, then the necessary 21st century transformative leaders will emerge.

***There seems to be a deep flaw in our make-up:*** humans are enormously creative; we can mobilise ourselves rapidly when a threat becomes immediate, as in the case of WW2. Significantly, this war might have been prevented if we had acted differently many years beforehand. But we seem unable to react to long-term threats that are emerging slowly and the symptoms are not yet catastrophic. Remember the frogs in the slowly heating pot? And in this case, as argued above, it could be too late. We know that the longer we delay, the more costly it will be – see more in Chapter 4: *A fatally flawed mind-set.*

***We have another flawed pattern – abdicating responsibility***. We say *"It's the Government's job"* or *"It's China that's the problem"*. Therefore, we do nothing. Clearly if everyone is playing that game, nothing will happen – other than increasingly extreme disaster. The truth is that all of us have to accept responsibility.

It is now almost 22 years since the first United Nations Conference on Environment and Development was held in Rio de Janeiro in June 1992. The 2010 Cancun agreement stated that future global warming should be limited to below 2.0 °C relative to the pre-industrial level. But the agreement had no legal force; there was no decisive action. The big nations did not want to give up their competitive advantage.

**bruce nixon**

Political and business leaders, meeting at UN Summits and G8 and G20 gatherings for all these years, whilst the situation has steadily worsened, have so far proved incapable of decisive action to tackle these threats. They have failed us taxpayers who pay for these costly jamborees.

Whilst international action is needed, without it, the best way forward is for nations to act independently in ways that do not adversely affect their economies but in fact benefit them.

***There is no shortage of solutions.*** We could easily develop the power and heating we need from renewable sources without resorting to nuclear energy *and* leave most of the remaining oil and coal in the ground. We could easily provide sustainable transport and get more people out of their cars and onto their feet or bicycles, thus improving their health. We could easily create beautiful sustainable, affordable and happier mixed housing developments. It just requires the political courage, will and citizen power to demand it. Countries like Germany, Denmark, Sweden and Norway are far ahead of Britain. Some technologies need more research and development. As they are used on a wider scale, they become cheaper. New, as yet unthought-of technologies will be developed. *Oxford in 2065* provides an exciting vision of how city areas could be by 2065. Some of it is already happening. This is the kind of vision we need; this is what can inspire nations (*Oxford in 2065* by Taissa Csaky and Richard Lofthouse in Oxford Today – duckduckgo.com/?q=oxford+in+2065&ia =maps).

## the 21st century revolution

Invaluable assessments of combinations of a variety of solutions are provided in Professor David Mackay's *Sustainable Energy – without the hot air* (www.withouthotair.com/Synopsis.html). His book provides detailed information about the emissions from different sources such as energy industries, transport, manufacturing, housing, agriculture, etc. Most useful are CO2 per passenger km. At the time of publication, the CO2 per passenger km for a Range Rover was well above a Boeing 747 and close to an ocean liner! Of course, the number of passengers must be taken into account. The biggest potential for saving emissions will come from reduced waste of energy. This makes nonsense of George Osborne's cancellation of the Green Levy.

**Oil supply, climate shock and financial collapse threaten tomorrow's economies.** Jeremy Leggett in his book, *The Energy of Nations*, describes how the systemic risks of oil supply, climate shock and financial collapse threaten tomorrow's economies and mean businesses and policy makers face formidable challenges in fuelling tomorrow's world. He describes the dangers often ignored and incompletely understood – the institutionalisation of denial and the reasons civilisations fail. It is also an account of hope, because mobilising renewables and redeploying energy funding can soften the crash of modern capitalism and set us on a road to renaissance.

It does not help if we get downhearted. Here are some good reasons to be hopeful and bring you cheer.

### *Reasons to be hopeful*

1. **Growth in Global CO2 emissions "stalled" in 2014**, according to the International Energy Agency (IEA). It is the first time in 40 years that annual CO2 emissions growth has remained stable, in the absence of a major economic crisis, the agency said. But the IEA warned that while the results were *"encouraging"*, this was *"no time for complacency"*. Professor Corinne Le Quere, Tyndall Centre for Climate Change Research, said: *"It provides much-needed momentum to negotiators preparing to forge a global climate deal in Paris in December; for the first time, greenhouse gas emissions are decoupling from economic growth."*
2. **China.** China's greenhouse gas emissions are likely to peak in 2025 (or even earlier), five years before its stated target, after which emissions will decline, according to research carried out by climate economist, Nicholas Stern, and analyst, Fergus Green, at the London School of Economics (LSE). Chinese coal consumption fell in 2014 and in the first quarter of 2015. This was caused by structural changes in the economy as well as government policies targeting more sustainable growth with a reduced environmental impact and air pollution (www.lse.ac.uk/GranthamInstitute/wp-content/uploads/2015/05/Boyd_et_al_policy_paper_May_2015.pdf)
3. But, worryingly, India seeks to open more and more coalmines to fuel growth.
4. **Barack Obama has made climate change one of his defining issues.** His revised *Clean Power Plan*

## the 21st century revolution

aims to cut carbon emissions from the power sector by 32% by 2030, compared with 2005 levels, by increasing wind and solar power and other renewable energy sources, and emission caps on coal power stations. At climate talks in New York, he promised the US would play a leading role in reaching an international agreement to fight climate change in Paris. President Barack Obama and China's President Xi Jinping have made pledges on greenhouse gas emissions at talks in Beijing. They agreed to make sure that international climate change negotiations reached an agreement in Paris in 2015. With Barack Obama as its champion, and Hilary Clinton, if elected, committed to defending the plan, there is potential for making the Presidential Election a referendum on climate change action.

5. **Pope Francis**, leader of an estimated 1.2 billion Roman Catholics, calls for a radical transformation of politics, economics and individual lifestyles to confront environmental degradation and climate change. His critique of consumerism and irresponsible development with a plea for swift and unified global action is to be welcomed. In his 184-page papal encyclical, he describes relentless exploitation and destruction of the environment and says apathy, the reckless pursuit of profits, excessive faith in technology and political short-sightedness are to blame. The most vulnerable victims are the world's poorest people, who are being dislocated and disregarded.

6. **Paul Polman**, Head of Unilever, called on world leaders to raise their game in the battle against

climate change. He urged governments to set clear CO2 targets to force low-carbon innovation. Ahead of a business climate summit in Paris, he urged fellow chief executives to help create a *"political licence"* for politicians to promote clean energy. *"It's clear that, increasingly, the business community is aware of the costs of climate change. Momentum is swinging towards people realising that we need to take urgent action to stay below two degrees [increase in global average temperature]."* (BBC News)

7. **Divestment.** People are taking their money out of fossil fuels. Dozens of cities, institutions and investors, including leaders of churches, are taking their money out of fossil fuel companies after the launch of a divestment campaign in the US around 18 months ago. Glasgow became the first university in Europe to divest from fossil fuels. UUniversity court voted to divest £18m from fossil fuel industry in what campaigners call a "dramatic beachhead". Heirs to Rockefeller Standard Oil fortune have joined the campaign to withdraw a total of $50bn from fossil fuels, including from tar sands funds.

8. ***Global investment in clean energy*** rose by 16% in 2014, boosted by fast-growing solar power in the US and China. New figures from Bloomberg New Energy Finance (BNEF) show $310bn (£205bn) was invested in green energy last year, just short of the record $317bn in 2011. Solar, whose costs have fallen dramatically in recent years, attracted over half the total. As green energy gets ever cheaper, the money invested in 2014 bought almost double the clean electricity capacity than in 2011. Bloomberg

New Energy Finance estimates that, by 2030, spending on renewable energy sources could make up two-thirds of a global energy spend of US $7.7 trillion. Already, 22% of world energy is produced by renewables.

9. ***Solar Energy.*** The International Energy Agency (IEA) says the price of installing photovoltaic (solar electricity) systems dropped by two-thirds over the past six years. The resulting solar explosion has generated a *"prosumer"* market, in which the owners of homes and businesses are taking ownership of a growing proportion of the energy supply. In the UK, almost 5GW of solar energy capacity was installed in 2014, up from 2.8GW by the end of 2013 – enough low-carbon power to supply the equivalent of 1.5m homes. 650,000 solar installations were built for homes, offices, schools, churches, warehouses, farms, police stations, train stations, and even a bridge. The statistics reflect steady growth in the UK solar industry and rapidly falling costs (Department of Energy and Climate Change (DECC)).

10. ***Heat Flow Energy.*** The UK Department for Energy and Climate Change says that a new online tool for communities has revealed that at least one million homes and businesses across England could be tapping into clean, renewable heat embodied in the country's waterways, lakes and seas.

11. ***Bangladeshi women are being retrained as solar technicians.*** Bangladeshi women, who previously lived without electricity, have been retraining as solar technicians to bring power to the country's 95 million people who live without electric light. The

country now has the fastest growing solar sector in the world, with two million households fitted with solar power units.

12. ***European homes are using 15% less energy than they were in 2000.*** In every part of the world (barring the Middle East), governments are taking advantage of the cheapest way to bring down their emissions – by saving energy. Energy efficient housing and appliances have reduced global household emissions by almost 1% per year, equivalent to every resident of New York going completely off grid. In the EU, households reduced their consumption by 15.5% between 2000 and 2011.

13. ***Cutting emissions is good for business.*** Recently, WWF/Ceres reported 53 US Fortune 100 companies had cut their carbon footprint by 58 million megatons in 2012 – roughly equivalent to the total emissions of Peru. This was achieved mainly through energy efficiency measures, although switching to green energy sources was a factor. Each megaton reduction saved an average of US $19 – a total of US $1.1 billion across 53 companies. In the UK, tyre manufacturer Michelin has reduced its £20 million energy bill by 20% in five years by employing energy managers.

14. ***Oil is becoming much more expensive to find.*** Oil and gas companies are finding it increasingly expensive to find and extract their buried gravy. The total capital expenditure of Chevron, Exxon Mobil and Royal Dutch Shell grew to £70 billion in 2013, but all three experienced large declines in

production relative to cost. Off the coast of Brazil, great oil fields lie over five kilometres beneath the ocean floor. However, deep drilling in the oceans and the costs of exploring the Arctic are proving so high that many companies have withdrawn or shelved such exploration.

15. ***Electric car sales are doubling each year.*** Since 2011, electric car sales have doubled every year. Consumer acceptance is growing exponentially and researchers expect over a million electric vehicles will be driven in the world by the end of 2015. In Norway, one in every hundred cars is now electric. Currently, the USA has 174,000 electric cars, Japan 68,000, and China 45,000. Battery technology is developing.

16. ***Younger people are buying fewer cars***, choosing to live closer together and use mobile phones to communicate (Quartz – qz.com/337398/the-western-world-has-turned-its-back-on-car-culture).

17. ***Storage for Renewable Energy.*** Elon Musk, CEO of Tesla Motors, has announced production of batteries that can power homes and businesses. It has enormous potential as the world moves away from fossil fuels and to energy sources like solar and wind. Prices will come down with development, increased sales and competition. However, the lithium ion battery may supersede other technology, like hydrogen fuel cells. Friends of the Earth's renewable energy campaigner, Alasdair Cameron, says having solar panels and a home battery in the future could become as common as central

heating (thanks to the BBC – www.bbc.co.uk/news/technology-32545081).

18. ***Hydrogen fuel cell vehicles.*** Toyota, Hyundai and Honda are developing and launching hydrogen fuel cell vehicles. Ford has put $1.3m into a fleet of fuel cell vehicles and recently combined with Daimler, Renault and Nissan to develop a joint fuel cell technology that all four companies would share. General Motors, which holds more patents for hydrogen fuel cell technology than any other carmaker, has tested its HydroGen4 car and is working with Honda to develop new fuel cell applications. Fuel cell vehicles address the two main shortcomings of current battery-powered cars: short driving range and long recharging times. The latest news is that Graphene could revolutionise the development of electric cars and green energy by extracting hydrogen fuel from air with no damaging waste products. Nobel Prize winner, Professor Sir Andrei Geim, of Manchester University, who is leading this research, stresses that it is in early stages.

19. ***Brazil.*** 48% of its energy matrix is renewable, mostly thanks to hydropower, the source of 80% of the electricity consumed in the country. However, the process of producing ethanol, which has been powering vehicles in the country since the late 1970s, produces considerable pollution and competes with food crops. Their record with deforestation is not so admirable and they are beginning to face water shortages.

20. ***Retro-fitting homes.*** Over 100,000 homes in UK could be given a carbon-neutral retrofit by 2020 if the

EU approves funding. Pilot projects could start within a year on council estates and housing association properties in London, Birmingham and southern England that would save 1,950 GWh of energy. The Energiesprong (Energy Leap) initiative involves wrapping houses with insulated panel-facades. Insulated roofs with high-efficiency solar panels are fastened on top; heat pumps, hot water storage tanks and ventilation units are put in garden sheds.

21. ***Solar lighting replaces harmful kerosene lighting within Africa.*** Jeremy Leggett reports that the social enterprise, SolarAid/Sunny Money, have sold 1.5 million solar lights. That has brought clean, good quality solar light to around nine million people in fifty-four African countries. We have a fighting chance of achieving our mission now: a lead role in eradicating kerosene use in lighting from the whole of Africa as soon as 2020 (theelders.org/article/economic-case-against-fossil-fuel).

22. ***Local Power.*** Local authorities, communities and schools plan to generate their own power. Plymouth, Nottingham, Bristol and Berwickshire local authorities are planning to set up as electricity and gas retailers, offering significantly lower charges than the big six. In the longer-term, many plan to produce their energy through renewable sources such as wind and solar. Eight Scottish housing associations and a renewable energy charity are close to signing a financing deal to supply power to thousands of households. Transition Towns are also setting up community power schemes. The same

process is happening in USA. Similarly, communal food growing schemes are being created.
23. **Tidal Lagoons.** Plans have been announced to generate electricity from the world's first series of tidal lagoons in the UK. Six lagoons – four in Wales and one each in Somerset and Cumbria – will capture incoming and outgoing tides behind giant sea walls, and use the weight of the water to power turbines. The £1bn Swansea scheme, expected to produce energy for 155,000 homes, is already in the planning system. The cost of generating power from the Swansea project will be very high, but subsequent lagoons should be able to produce electricity much more cheaply. Six lagoons could generate 8% of the UK's electricity for an investment of £30bn. The £90-£95 per MWh for power from a second, more efficient lagoon in Cardiff, will compare favourably with the £92.50 price for power from the planned Hinkley nuclear station, especially as the lagoon is designed to last 120 years – at a much lower risk than nuclear (Source: www.bbc.co.uk/news/science-environment-31682529).
24. **The UK National Trust** has just announced a new £1bn, 10-year plan. Decades of intensive farming and the loss of habitat have sent wildlife numbers tumbling, with 60% of species declining in the UK over the last 50 years. The National Trust has pledged to try to reverse this decline, through its own actions and working with partners, hundreds of tenant farmers among its estates, as well as woodland, beauty spots, coastline, rivers and historic properties. This will benefit farmers, the economy and the environment,

> provide more habitats for birds, animals and insects, and protect fragile soils under threat from erosion. With more than 4.2 million members and about 20 million visitors each year, many from overseas, it could have a considerable influence.
>
> The idea for this table, with my additions, is based on Karl Mathiesen's article in the Guardian.com, 30th July 2014, *10 Reasons to be hopeful that we will overcome climate change* (www.theguardian.com/environment/2014/jul/30/reasons-hopeful-overcome-climate-change-solar). Also thanks to www.onehundredmonths.org.

**Nuclear power is not a solution.** It will take too long to come on-stream, cost too much, and the Government will have to insure the unknown and potentially catastrophic risks (www.world-nuclear.org/info/Current-and-Future-Generation/The-Nuclear-Debate/), as we have recently seen in Fukushima (fukushimaupdate.com). We have yet to find a sure way of disposing safely of nuclear waste. We would leave a toxic legacy for future generations. And imagine the scope nuclear power generation provides for terrorists.

**The key decision we need to make.** We have to face that the only effective solution, as usual, is to go upstream, and decide to leave fossil fuels in the ground.

*"A third of oil reserves, half of gas reserves, and over 80% of current coal reserves globally should remain in the ground and not be used before 2050 if global warming is to stay below the 2°C target agreed by policy makers. The overwhelming majority of the huge coal reserves in China,*

*Russia and the United States should remain unused. The Middle East should also leave over 60% of its gas reserves in the ground. The development of resources in the Arctic and any increase in unconventional oil are also inconsistent with efforts to limit climate change."* (UCL Institute for Sustainable Resources [www.bartlett.ucl.ac.uk/sustainable/sustainable-news/nature_fossil_fuels](www.bartlett.ucl.ac.uk/sustainable/sustainable-news/nature_fossil_fuels)).

This too makes nonsense of the UK Government's policies.

# Chapter 4

# A fatally flawed mind-set

A central theme of this book is the need for whole systems thinking. In this chapter, I describe examples of attempts to solve problems without seeing them as parts of an overall system and the consequences for the whole system are not taken into account. I give an example in which the biggest challenges facing humanity were left out.

Politics is often described as the art of the possible; I say it is the art of the impossible.

> *"It always seems impossible until it is done."*
> **Nelson Mandela**

The greatest threat to our survival is the way our brains are wired. We see what we want to see and screen out what we don't. We turn a blind eye to inconvenient information.

*"Human evolution makes us suited to dealing with a charging elephant, but not capable of properly reacting to or preparing for a danger years down the line. ... Politicians have been allowed by the public to make grand speeches about the threat as long as they do not interfere with the lifestyle of people who are knowingly destroying their own life-support system."* (**Paul Brown**, reviewing George

### bruce nixon

Marshall's book, *Don't Even Think About it: Why Our Brains Are Wired To Ignore Climate Change. Putting our heads in the sand, Resurgence Ecologist*, March/April 2015.)

**New Runways.** In May 2014, the news media was full of the debate about whether a new runway should be built at Heathrow or Gatwick. It is all about the assumed growing need for air travel – as if we have no choice – still below 2007 levels, the need to compete with other countries, cost benefit analysis and compensation for, rather than reduction of, noise and air pollution.

The International Air Transport Association (IATA), in its first 20-year passenger growth forecast, projected that passenger numbers are expected to reach 7.3 billion by 2034. That represents a 4.1% average annual growth in demand for air connectivity that will result in more than a doubling of the 3.3 billion passengers expected to travel this year (www.iata.org/pressroom/pr/pages/2014-10-16-01.aspx). Global aviation produces about 2% of all human emissions, 12% of all transport sources, and they are particularly harmful.

The UK Climate Change Act 2008, to prevent global temperatures from rising by more than 2°C, made it the duty of the Secretary of State to ensure that the net UK carbon account for all six Kyoto greenhouse gases for the year 2050 is at least 60% lower than the 1990 baseline by 2050. Emissions from aviation and shipping were provisionally excluded, that to be reviewed in 2016. Environmental organisations and some political parties criticise the 60% target as being insufficiently ambitious, and are demanding greater cuts (80%-100%).

## the 21st century revolution

We know that flying is one of the most environmentally damaging ways to travel; short-haul flights do more damage per passenger kilometres than long-haul. Aircraft emissions, and air and noise pollution, pose a major problem. The efficiency of aircraft is steadily increasing. But this will be insignificant. We need to do everything we can to reduce the harmful effects on our planet and human health, especially by cutting unnecessary flying. It is the Government's responsibility to do everything possible to minimise flying and develop sustainable alternatives, especially for shorter journeys.

Yet the debate about a third runway at Heathrow, as reported, makes no mention of this imperative. It's all about accommodating more passengers and competing with other European countries. This is crazy, given the predictions about our climate and the fact that we are consuming the Earth's resources at an unsustainable rate. In fact, if we are to save ourselves, we need to collaborate, not complete. Construction of this runway alone would have an enormous eco-footprint, apart from the increased pollution.

The Government-appointed Airports Commission, headed by Sir Howard Davies, was not asked the overwhelmingly most important question: *How can we reduce flying?*

Also, did he get the whole system into the room, namely people who are climate experts, ecologists and holistic scientists? This is another extraordinary example of blinkered thinking and not giving intelligent people the correct brief. I suggest this:

**bruce nixon**

*What transport system does the UK need in order to combat climate change and support its goals – namely a prosperous economy, providing good work, wellbeing and health for everyone?*

First, we need to define the goals of the economy, namely the wellbeing of all humanity and the Earth on which all life depends including us.

The £17bn estimated cost of the third runway would go a long way towards building safe cycle lanes all over the country and encouraging people to get out of their cars. That would certainly reduce greenhouse emissions, as well as deadly pollution and road crashes. Once again, it would also improve health and help reduce the multi-billion NHS bill for obesity, heart disease, strokes, diabetes and cancer. Prevention is always better and cheaper than cure. Electrifying and enlarging the whole rail system, providing better transport links between and within Northern cities and towns and better local bus services would offer similar benefits.

There will be no economy unless we tackle climate change and our destruction of the ecosystem.

**Next, the Government announces a £30bn road-building plan.** They are trying to push through an Infrastructure Bill that would make road-building much easier, with a "climate-gag" clause, making it harder for local communities to object citing increases in carbon emissions. It is well-known that such measures increase road traffic, ultimately cause more congestion, and take people away from our too costly railways. That adds to the

## the 21st century revolution

already high air pollution that is contributing to 28,000 premature deaths annually and 7 million worldwide. A study in 2007 estimated the costs to society in UK at £12-£18 per annum.

This sum – altogether £47bn (17bn plus 30bn) – would be far better spent on rail transport, electrifying the whole system, improvements for cyclists and encouraging people to walk (in a later chapter I'll explain how money can be provided for infrastructure without incurring debt). Research carried out for Campaign for Better Transport found that HGVs pay less than 40% of the costs associated with their activities, with the taxpayer picking up the rest of the bill.

It highlights that HGVs do not pay for their impacts on congestion, road infrastructure, public health or the natural environment. More than half (52%) of fatal accidents on motorways involve HGVs, despite HGVs only making up 10% of motorway traffic; HGVs are involved in one in five fatal crashes on A-roads, a ratio that has worsened over the last 5 years; a HGV is five times as likely to be involved in a fatal accident on a minor road than other traffic.

**HS2 – The proposed high speed rail link between London and Birmingham.** Has this highly controversial scheme been properly justified? The New Economics Foundation's report said:

*"We are on the verge of the biggest transport investment in UK history. With a cost to taxpayers of £33bn, High Speed 2 (HS2)'s massive price tag is almost too big to visualise –*

*which might explain how it has got this far without more public concern.*

*The economic case for major infrastructure investment is clear, and you certainly can't fault HS2 on its objectives. £33 billion spent on fixing Britain's skewed economic geography and making our transport greener and more resilient is £33 billion well spent in anyone's books – if it works.*

*But is wise to plough such huge sums on a single project when spreading the same budget across many smaller, more robust schemes would positively transform the UK's broader transport landscape? Do we really want to spend 20 years waiting for the HS2 line to inch into shape when there are numerous shovel-ready, targeted options that could (a) be rolled out in a fraction of the time, (b) benefit more people across a wider area, and (c) beat HS2 at its own objectives? We cannot know for sure without a proper appraisal process."* (Is HS2 really the best way to spend £33bn?)

If you want better and sustainable transport, support the Better Transport Campaign ([www.bettertransport.org.uk](www.bettertransport.org.uk)).

In Chapter 7, I'll explain how money required for infrastructure could be provided, without incurring debt, through Sovereign Money ([www.positivemoney.org/our-proposals/sovereign-money-creation](www.positivemoney.org/our-proposals/sovereign-money-creation)). Meanwhile, much of it could be funded out of the roughly £40bn of VAT, income tax, national insurance and corporation tax lost to the UK Exchequer every year (official figures).

## the 21st century revolution

During the run-up to the European Parliament election, I read the campaign leaflets of MEP candidates. The two largest parties made no mention of climate change. Clearly, they judged it not a vote-winner. That was left to the Lib Dems and Greens. This is typical: putting party interests before the interests of the nation and the survival of human beings on the planet. How can our supposed leaders be so short-sighted and irresponsible? They are failing to provide statesmanship and political courage at this critical moment in human history. Worse still, according to reports of the Tory and Labour party conferences in autumn, there was little or no mention of climate change. Why are they seemingly incapable of thinking about future generations?

**Fossil fuel subsidies.** Another example of folly is when we should be leaving oil and coal in the ground.

*"The UK is spending £12 billion every year on energy subsidies, the vast majority of which goes to the fossil fuel industry, directly or indirectly. Subsidies for renewable energy are a fraction in comparison."* The Politics of Climate Change, **Caroline Lucas MP**, *Resurgence & Ecologist*, July/August 2014.

Fossil fuel subsidies reached $90 billion in the OECD and over $500 billion globally in 2011. Renewable energy subsidies reached $88 billion in 2011. According to Fatih Birol, Chief Economist at the International Energy Agency, without a phasing out of fossil fuel subsidies, we will not reach our climate targets (Wikipedia – en.wikipedia.org/wiki/Energy_subsidies).

### bruce nixon

All this is madness. These are examples of the Government and political leaders' inability to think about the whole system and the long-term – to be fair, that applies to most of us. The obsession with economic growth, measured by GDP (Gross Domestic Product), is equally mad, bearing in mind that we live on a finite planet and GDP is not a measure of happiness or wellbeing – more on this later.

**"Climate change is not a future thing, it is already happening."** Juxtaposed on the same day is NASA's (National Aeronautics and Space Administration) report that key glaciers in West Antarctica are in an irreversible retreat. NASA says six big ice streams are draining into the Amundsen Bay and concludes that nothing now can stop them melting away. If the glaciers disappear, they would add roughly 1.2m to global sea levels. Imagine that! They add that these are abrupt events and the timescales involved are likely to be measured in centuries. However, as *The Observer* (Sunday, 18th May 2014) points out, scientists are cautious and most of their evaluations are likely to be underestimates. And, *"Climate change is not a future thing, it is already happening."* People in in low-lying places, like Miami, Bangladesh and Kiribati know this well. Initially, the hardest hit will be the poorest countries.

Our Parliament lies low beside the Thames. I keep getting this image: water from the Thames flows gently across the carpet of the House of Commons as the Prime Minister and the Leader of the Opposition slag each other off, competing for who is wittiest in this childish joust. Suddenly they wake up to reality and the Speaker shouts, *"All out! Get into the boats."*

## the 21st century revolution

The consequences of Climate Chaos are happening all over the world; delay will be vastly more costly in money and lives than if we take radical action now.

It is criminally irresponsible for governments to neglect this threat. Ultimately, it will be seen for what it is: a crime against humanity.

**The In/Out referendum on EU membership** is another leadership folly at a time when European collaboration on climate change is essential. It's sabre rattling. Whilst extensive reform and a radical re-think is essential, taking the long view, the European collaboration has brought many benefits to 500 million people, not least freedom from world war for 75 years. Today, collaboration between European nations is essential to meet the challenges of climate change, including exploiting the benefits of integrated energy systems for the whole area from the North Sea to the Mediterranean (www.theguardian.com/commentisfree/2014/may/18/european-elections-benefits-of-eu-need-for-change).

**Debate about immigration** is another example of a dysfunctional mind-set. On this subject and many others, there is an excess of dramatic headlines and a paucity of facts based on reliable research. Being an admired, multi-cultural society, we have a world influence far in excess of our puny global size. The successful solution of great world problems such as climate change, migration, planetary destruction and a dysfunctional global economy has a lot to do with inclusivity and the integration of international perspectives and ideas.

#### bruce nixon

*"We need more than politics as usual when it comes to immigration; we need reasoned, thoughtful, compassionate debate that focuses on our hopes, not our fears."* **President Barack Obama**

He has used his powers to allow illegal immigrants with American children to work and pay their taxes legally.

Growing inequality, populist politicians and alarmist media raise public anxieties. Instead of fuelling ill-informed debate, political leaders need to give leadership, provide the public with reliable facts, and introduce measures to support communities affected by short-term local costs. Badly-thought–out, short-term fixes risk undermining the growth and dynamism of the British economy. Caps on migrants fail to control population or promote British jobs and economic growth (Centre for Research and Analysis of Migration, University College London). It is estimated that migrants contributed £20bn to the UK economy between 2001 and 2011.

The benefits of immigration outweigh the costs. The Office for Budget Responsibility forecasts suggest that the faster recovery claimed by George Osborne has much to do with the contribution of immigrants. Migrants from the EU pay significantly more in taxes – an extra £8bn, according to the Institute of Fiscal Studies – than they claim in benefits or education, health or other expenditures. There is no basis for fears that immigrants undermine job prospects or reduce wages in UK or any other major economy. Immigrants tend to be "exceptional people" who strive to overcome adversity. The diversity they bring serves as a catalyst that spurs creativity and performance. This is as true in business

## the 21st century revolution

as it is in academia, medicine, science, politics, arts, food, culture, entertainment and sports. Unskilled migrants do jobs local workers will not do, such as agricultural labour. By providing affordable child-minding, they allow a greater share of women to participate in the workforce.

*"Properly managed immigration does not pose a threat to the UK. What we need is an adult debate that looks at the UK and global evidence. Immigration is too important to be crushed under the weight of populist politics."* **Professor Ian Goldin**

This source for this is *More immigration – but managed much better. That's what the UK needs*, by Professor Ian Goldin, Director of the Oxford Martin School at the University of Oxford, published in *The Observer*, Sunday 9th November 2014 ([www.theguardian.com/commentisfree/2014/nov/09/increase-immigration-manage-it-better](www.theguardian.com/commentisfree/2014/nov/09/increase-immigration-manage-it-better)).

**Fracking.** In the Queen's speech, a bill was announced to enable fracking under people's houses when we should be going all out to invest in renewable energy. This will just put that day off. It is another shocking example of the Government's criminal irresponsibility and favouring big business above the interests of people. All the pomp and ceremony, the good Queen arriving in a gilded fairy-tale coach with electric windows, with people in fancy dress, seemed not only ridiculous but insensitive when so many people are suffering from austerity.

Political leaders, national and international, are failing us. There is enormous frustration about this. It is not that we don't know what to do. We're simply not doing it.

### bruce nixon

***It's not just Climate Chaos.*** We need to remember five equally important key issues:
- Climate Chaos, Peak Oil, Peak Everything
- The rapid destruction of the ecosystem on which all life, including our own, depends
- Economic injustice, poverty and the growing gap between the very rich and the rest
- Resolving conflict without violence
- Radical reform of broken and corrupt, top-down politics

These issues are *inter-related* and will be fully explored in later chapters.

***Human beings are amazingly adaptive and creative.*** That's how we've survived. However, it has to be said that we are not good at seeing the big picture or thinking about the long-term. And now that could be fatal. We have a strange way of compartmentalising our thinking. For example, we know that speed kills and we do everything we can to protect our children. Yet we ignore the speed limit, drive recklessly, tailgate drivers who stick to the limit, beep them angrily, and buy swanky cars capable of much more than 100 mph, even though there are no roads in the UK on which we can legally drive at that speed. Young people, often soon after passing their test and with little experience, kill or maim themselves and their friends by demonstrating their prowess as fast drivers.

***We know what's to be done***; many practical solutions already exist; alternative technologies are being steadily developed and becoming cheaper every day; other solutions, currently undreamed of, will be invented by

### the 21st century revolution

mavericks like Sir Timothy John and Tim Berners-Lee (honoured as the *"Inventor of the World Wide Web"*) during 2012, and Sebastian Burkhard Thrun, former Director of the Stanford Artificial Intelligence Laboratory and co-inventor of Google Street View, who initially headed Google's self-driving car project. The discoveries of coal, and later oil, brought about industrial revolutions.

**Countless medical advances** are transforming our chances of long and healthy lives. Stem-cell transplants offer hope of a cure for blindness. At last, there is hope for people paralysed by spinal injuries. Professor Geoff Raisman of UCL, who has spent his career pursuing the dream of spinal cord regeneration, discovered that the nerve cells in the lining of the nose constantly renew themselves. Darek Fidyka was paralysed from the chest down after being stabbed. Dr Pawel Tabakow, head of a team of Polish scientists in Wroclaw, performed delicate surgery to open his skull, remove one of Darek's olfactory bulbs, at the base of the brain, and a second operation to expose the damaged spinal cord and transplant the cells. Darek Fidyka can now walk with the aid of a frame. Dr Tabakow is now pioneering a new technique to remove olfactory bulbs through the nose, a far less invasive procedure. All this work is made possible by the Nicholls Spinal Injuries Foundation, started by David Nicholls, whose 18-year-old son was paralysed in a swimming accident. He promised his son would walk again. So far, over £2.5m has been raised (thanks to Fergus Walsh, BBC medical correspondent – www.bbc.co.uk/news/health-29686709).

There will be many more transformative inventions as great, or greater, than these.

### bruce nixon

**Practical, innovative ideas** are being discovered and implemented all over the world (*An optimist's tour of the future* by Mark Stevenson – anoptimiststourofthefuture.com). Individuals and local communities can bring about many of the necessary changes – Transition Towns are one of many bottom-up initiatives (www.transitionnetwork.org and www.transitionnetwork.org/support/what-transition-initiative). Many of these innovations will make products cheaper, take production away from large, industrial companies, and put production and services into the hands of individuals and local communities. They could take power away from central government and put power into the hands of communities. But, misused, they could make a few people even richer and lead to even greater abuses of power. We know power corrupts. George Orwell's *Nineteen Eighty-Four* could become reality.

**A third industrial revolution is on its way.** Jeremy Rifkin describes how a third industrial revolution may already be taking place that will precipitate the eclipse of capitalism in its present form.

*"We are just beginning to glimpse the bare outlines of an emerging, new economic system – the collaborative commons."* **Jeremy Rifkin**, author of *The Zero Marginal Cost Society: The Internet of Things, the Collaborative Commons, and the Eclipse of Capitalism*.

He says the zero-marginal cost revolution is beginning to initiate profound change through an emerging, general-purpose technology platform – the internet of things. The convergence of the communications internet with the fledgling renewable energy internet and automated logistics internet in a smart, inter-operable internet-of-things system is giving rise to a third industrial revolution. We may have the benefit of very much cheaper or even free products because of zero marginal cost. New body parts may be possible to heal fatal or life-threatening diseases, undo the results of devastating injuries, and improve our lives in old age (see bigthink.com/think-tank/the-collaborative-commons-economy).

**The largest movement in history.** There is a revolution in thinking about the fundamentals of our society. In his book, *Blessed Unrest – How the largest social movement in history is restoring grace, justice and beauty to the world*, Peter Hawken reckoned there may be as many as a million such organisations in 243 countries, some of which are available on the Wiser Earth website (www.wiserearth.org). As I shall report later, there is demand from students for fresh thinking about economics (The International Student Initiative for Pluralist Economics (ISIPE) – www.isipe.net).

**Transformative leadership is needed.** Governments have a major role: providing an environmental and economic strategy for businesses to fulfil, support for research, large-scale infrastructure, and enabling laws and legislation and taxation and subsidies to prevent harms and foster goods. Governments need to collaborate at regional, e.g. European, and international levels. Withdrawal from the EU makes no sense. We urgently need far-sighted leadership, not a leadership obsessed with power, the latest headlines and the next election. Again, we need a completely different kind of leadership that serves the nation, leaders who have integrity and enable people to empower themselves. It's called **Servant-Leadership** (www.greenleaf.org.uk).

**Mind-set is the problem.** How likely is this leadership to come from current political class? Their minds are stuck an old paradigm that is patently failing us. Currently, they are the problem, not the solution.

*"A problem is never solved by the same type of thinking that created it."* **Albert Einstein**

**A Great Global Power Shift.** Extraordinary *"ordinary people"* like you, dear reader, who are at the leading edge, must fill the gap. We are not destined to be victims; collectively seven billion people have enormous power. We have to mobilise ourselves and demand that our governments do what's necessary. It is already happening but it has to become more powerful. We have to provide governments with the mandate. George Barda of Global Power Shift says only 1-7% of the population are needed to create critical mass (globalpowershift.org).

**If we want a better world, we first need to transform ourselves.** None of these developments will be enough unless we face the underlying issue – namely ourselves. Technology alone will not solve our problems. The potential of technology is easily used as an excuse to continue on the same path. Without inner change, technological innovations could make things worse.

*"We share an urgent desire to find ways of being human, which aren't dependent on money."* **Lucy Purdy**, writing in Positive News

We need a change of heart, a profound change in our values and how we live with, not against, nature. We'll be happier. More stuff does not make us happier. The greatest happiness comes from simple things like love.

*"What you own ends up owning you,"* my son-in law said to me when I complained of being burdened and stressed with all the things I think I have to do.

*"The world has enough for everyone's need, but not enough for anyone's greed."* **Mahatma Gandhi**

We need to learn to collaborate, to value difference and diversity, welcome views different from our own and, above all, give up violence and war.

***Dreaming is the first step in transformation.*** People are moved by a vision of a better world, not by sacrifice, fear and gloom. We need to ***imagine*** a better future, as William Morris did in his far-sighted book, News from Nowhere. He influenced transformative leaders like the UK's post-war Prime Minister, Clement Attlee. It was a utopian future in which there was no poverty, houses were beautiful, and the filth of industrialisation was gone. People had fulfilling, rewarding work, more leisure, and enjoyed long lives in good health, looking youthful for many more years. In this society, there is no private property; there is common ownership and there is democratic control of the means of production. Many live communally. There are no big cities, no authority, no monetary system, no divorce, no courts, no prisons and no class system. This agrarian society functions simply because the people find pleasure in nature, and therefore they find pleasure in their work. Today, the promise of new technology, if used wisely, could make much of this possible. Few would agree with every aspect of William Morris's utopia but it is the essence of what many of us desire.

*I am an optimist*. Pessimism and cynicism are an indulgence; they affect or, should I say, infect other people. So does optimism. We a relational species; relating positively and lovingly is essential to our survival. How we are with others is contagious. That can work both ways – either encouraging positive action or re-enforcing powerlessness. We also imitate others. That can help us. Pioneers start the process that at first is pooh-poohed and angrily resisted; gradually, it spreads, gathers momentum, and becomes a transformation – as long as it does not become violent. So I see all these challenges as opportunities. Whist I have described the challenges without flinching, I believe we are presented with an opportunity to create a better world for everyone. What is being done to us is an outrage; we need to *feel* our outrage. We have been conditioned not to be passionate; that suits the ruling class. It is no good saying *"Don't be negative"*. We need to understand the system in order to understand how to change it. We also need to empower ourselves by imagining a far better future. Imagining is the starting point for any fundamental change.

### Hope

*"Everything that is done in the world is done by hope."*
**Dr Martin Luther King**

But it has to be the right kind of hope. It would be a foolish hope or belief that, on their current form, any of the current leaders in the main parties will save the situation.

## the 21st century revolution

That defies experience. Active hope, as defined by Chris Johnstone, co-author with Joanna Macy of *Active Hope* ([chrisjohnstone.info/active-hope](chrisjohnstone.info/active-hope)), is something we do. It begins with a clear view of reality. But as I have said before, current political leaders are preoccupied with winning elections. They do not think long-term. They are in the pockets of big businesses, the super-rich and armaments suppliers, advised by scientists who are not always independent or properly informed, supported by a media, largely owned by the super-rich.

So we seven billion people need to pressure them and take independent action ourselves. And if we do, the right kind of leaders will emerge. As new parliaments are elected and new governments are formed, citizens all over the world have new opportunities.

# Chapter 5

## Neoliberalism exposed

*"When the capital development of a country becomes a by-product of the activities of a casino, the job is likely to be ill-done."* **John Maynard Keynes**

*"The policies showed a lack of understanding of the fundamentals of modern macroeconomics, which call for expansionary monetary and fiscal policies in the face of an economic downturn."* **Joseph E. Stiglitz**,
former World Bank Chief Economist

This is the story of a most extraordinary takeover: the takeover of the minds of politicians, economists throughout the Western world by the architects of consumerism and Neoliberalism. But first, I want to talk about illiteracy on a grand scale.

**Economic illiteracy and incompetence.** We might expect our Government to be competent and know what they are doing. I have already described some of political leaders as economically, environmentally and ecologically illiterate. That may sound harsh, if not abusive; not my usual style. But I believe their incompetence needs to be widely understood. Similar policies are being imposed in continental Europe; it is not surprising Europe's economy is stagnating and young people are rebelling.

The Tory-led UK Coalition Government seized the opportunity provided by the financial crisis to impose their ideology on the nation. Voices against this were not loud enough. They delayed economic recovery and inflicted enormous and unnecessary damage on our nation, our social and cultural institutions, many smaller businesses, citizens, especially poorer people, women and young people. Above all, they neglected the most urgent threat to our survival – namely environmental catastrophe. And they largely got away with it.

I want to explain what Neoliberal ideology is. Probably only a minority of the population have heard of this doctrine. The Sub Prime mortgage crisis in the USA and the irresponsibility of banks in the USA and the UK precipitated the collapse. But this economic crisis was the inevitable result of Neoliberal policies, pursued over the past 35 years. Both the Conservative and New Labour governments pursued these policies. Yet New Labour has been blamed by the Tory-led Coalition. In fairness, Gordon Brown played a major part in responding to the crisis.

**At the end of World War Two**, most of the world signed up to a very progressive agenda. International institutions were established, aiming to prevent the repetition of international crises such as the 1929 financial collapse, the Great Depression and subsequent war. The two main thinkers behind these institutions were Harry Dexter White, one of Franklin Roosevelt's closest advisers, and John Maynard Keynes, whose thinking was influential until the

1980s. These achievements included the United Nations, the International Monetary Fund and the World Bank, created at Bretton Woods in 1944. Their mandate was to help prevent future conflicts by lending for reconstruction and development and by smoothing out temporary balance of payment problems. At that time, they were seen as progressive institutions. At the end of WW2 in Britain, there was widespread agreement about the kind of social contract that was needed. In 1945, Clement Attlee, with the help of William Beveridge and a team of exceptionally talented ministers, set up the British Welfare State. It was widely admired and similar schemes were adopted in many other countries. Passionate, visionary and pragmatic, Nye Bevan set up the National Health Service, widely admired to this day. The Clement Attlee government built the post-war consensus, based upon full employment, Keynesian policies, and a system of social services outlined in the wartime Beveridge Report. This settlement was broadly accepted by all parties until Margaret Thatcher became Prime Minister in 1979. She and Ronald Reagan began to sweep this social contract away (*Attlee: A Life in Politics* and *Nye* and *The Political Life of Aneurin Bevan*, both by Nicklaus Thomas-Symonds; en.wikipedia.org/wiki/Clement_Attlee).

**Two developments began to take over Western minds**: Consumerism and Neoliberalism. Eventually, their influence became almost worldwide. They combined to have disastrous consequences for people and planet. Neo-conservatism is another dangerous political movement born in the United States during the 1960s. Basically, it meant imposing US-style democracy on other nations, whether they liked it or not, by bombs if necessary.

## the 21st century revolution

**Consumerism** became an important part of post-war philosophy, especially in the USA. Freud's daughter, Anna, and his nephew, Edward Bernays, were enlisted to help influence people to become consumers of products that would keep the factories busy. Advertising, with subliminal messages, would create unending dissatisfaction with what people already had, and encourage them to buy the latest model to *"keep up with the Joneses"* (thanks to Wikipedia – en.wikipedia.org/wiki/Vance_Packard). Built-in obsolescence and easy credit were part of it. Vance Packard's *The Hidden Persuaders*, 1957, explores the use of consumer motivational research and other psychological techniques, including depth psychology and subliminal tactics, by advertisers to prey on our anxieties, manipulate our expectations and induce desire for products, particularly in post-war America. He identified eight *"compelling needs"* that advertisers promise products will fulfil; so strong that people are compelled to buy products to satisfy them. The book also explores the manipulative techniques of promoting politicians to the electorate too.

Margaret Thatcher's era of conviction politics continued the trend of *"a thin-spun, debased consumer society, the engines of which were vacuous acquisition and an obsession with celebrity"* (www.newstatesman.com/uk-politics/2009/02/margaret-thatcher-mrs-labour). Today, the pace of innovation, especially in new technology, is even more rapid and few things are built to last. This was explored in the BBC/Open University three-part series, *The Men Who Made Us Spend*, in which Jacques Peretti exposes what keeps us hooked on spending (www.open.edu/openlearn/whats-on/tv/ou-on-the-bbc-the-men-who-made-us-spend and www.theguardian.com/tv-and-radio/2014/

jul/14/the-made-who-made-us-spend-review). Spending is helped by constant targeted advertisements in social media and search engines.

**Neoliberalism.** Neoliberal ideology informed the policies of Ronald Reagan, Margaret Thatcher and Tony Blair. It explains almost every policy and intervention of the recent Coalition and current Tory government. Neoliberalism is associated with the Chicago school of economics and economists such as Milton Friedman. They emphasized reduced intervention from Government and generally rejected regulation in markets as inefficient, with the exception of central bank regulation of the money supply. Milton Friedman strongly influenced Ronald Reagan and Margaret Thatcher, both of whom began implementing these policies in the 80s. Neoliberal policies were also adopted by the World Trade Organisation, the International Monetary Fund, and the World Bank, who forced them on poor and developing countries, as a condition for loans, in the form of Structural Adjustment Programmes, with disastrous consequences. Loans created a huge debt burden and Structural Adjustment Programmes damaged education, health and other public services.

Essentially, Neoliberalism stands for economic liberalisation, free trade, open markets, privatization, shrinking the public sector, deregulation, minimising the role of trades unions, a *"flexible"* workforce, borrowing rather than using taxation to pay for infrastructure, and enhancing the role of the private sector in modern society.

Above all, Neoliberalism benefits the rich, those with capital, regardless of the cost to people, and the environment. Shareholders are not yet very competent in monitoring what big companies are up to. But that is beginning to change.

**Short-termism.** Amongst the consequences of Neoliberalism are: short-termism and failure to invest; the sort of cuts we are experiencing now; seeing employees as costs to be reduced rather than creators of wealth; outsourcing jobs; zero-hours contracts; an inflated housing market that benefits wealthy owners of property; tax avoidance by locating transnational corporations in tax-havens or low tax regimes. All of this harms *"hard working people"*.

**Education is the responsibility of the state.** Education is another area being damaged by Neoliberal dogma. Rather than preparing young people for happy and fulfilling lives, it has become focussed on equipping them for business; science is financed by the relevant industries; decisions are taken on the basis of what will most benefit big business and the super-rich.

Higher education is being marketised and treated as a commodity. Students borrow to pay for the nation's education. Instead of being funded by grants, universities are now being funded through increasingly high tuition fees. Student loans provided by Government conveniently appear as assets in the books and give the appearance of a reduction in public spending. It is estimated that, by 2020, graduates may be facing debt approaching £50,000, when young people are already facing difficulty in buying a home.

**bruce nixon**

Here I quote from *Tuition fees are a consumerist fallacy. Our students deserve better*, The Guardian, 5th August 2015, Stefan Collini, Professor of English Literature and Intellectual History at the University of Cambridge (www.theguardian.com/commentisfree/2015/aug/05/tuition-fees-students).

"Reports that tuition fees could soon pass £10,000 per year should not come as a surprise. The whole system is inherently flawed. Ours is an enormously wealthy country that can easily afford to support a high-quality system of public higher education. Society as a whole benefits from the investment by previous generations, and society as a whole, represented by those who have the means, should contribute to maintaining such benefits for future generations. We need to recognise that it is a fiction to treat a tuition fee as though it paid the actual costs of that student's education; those have been incurred by the institution, indeed by the world of learning as a whole, long in the past. ... The issue here is about the further entrenching of class privilege in education by driving the children of the less well-off into institutions that charge less, while increasing the concentration of children from already advantaged backgrounds in those universities that then most augment their advantages in later life."

A particularly worrying example of how our government has imposed major change based on Neoliberal ideology, stealthily and without a mandate, is The Health and Social Care Act 2012. It removed responsibility for the health of citizens from the Secretary of Health, which the post had carried since the inception of the NHS in 1948.

## the 21st century revolution

*The NHS is rated more highly than any other comparable healthcare system in the world.* It is the world's largest public-funded health service, employing 1.3m people, three-quarters of whom are women, with a budget of over £100bn a year, dealing with 1m patients every 36 hours. International studies give high ranking to the UK and low rankings to USA. It is ranked first for efficiency among 11 rich countries in 2014. The World Health Organisation ranked the US 38th out of 190 countries, in spite of highest expenditure per capita on healthcare. Seven out of ten people say their NHS is one of the best in the world and provides them with a good service. Evidence suggests that poor performance in the US is directly attributable to reliance on market mechanisms. Studies on both sides of the Atlantic find the effects of market mechanisms and privatisation on healthcare quality and equity are largely inconclusive or negative. Regulation is extremely difficult. Marketization undermines ethics and focusses on treatment and cure rather than prevention, so vital to human wellbeing, and in order to prevent escalating costs. Investment needs to be shifted upstream to prevent people needing healthcare. Early health education is needed.

Justification for the fundamental changes introduced by the Health and Social Care Act are ideological, not evidence-based. Frequent top-down reorganisations since 1980 have been extremely costly and have damaged morale and efficiency. The recurring costs of market mechanisms have been conservatively estimated at £4.5bn annually, enough to pay for 10 specialised hospitals, 174,798 extra nurses, 42,413 extra GPs or 39,473,684 extra visits to A&E. PFI contracts begun by New Labour and continued by the

Coalition have resulted in huge 30-year financial burdens on the NHS.

Whilst needs are rising more steeply as a result of recession and austerity, funding has been constrained more than at any time since its foundation in 1948. It is estimated that the NHS faces a funding gap of £30 billion between now and 2020/21. There is a growing belief that the key to delivering a better service is leadership that *enables* staff to create solutions and innovate, rather than top-down reorganisation and privatisation.

Now the freedom to choose NHS providers is under threat from the Transatlantic Trade and Investment Partnership (discussed earlier in Chapter 2). Competitive open market healthcare is widely opposed by professional bodies and the majority of the public. Most people have little understanding of the changes, though they know that privatisation is taking place and they expect the outcomes to be worse for patients (Source: *The wrong medicine*, Anna Coote, New Economics Foundation (NEF) – www.neweconomics.org/publications/entry/the-wrong-medicine)

**Fundamental change without a mandate.** How can we, in a democracy, allow a government to make such fundamental changes, covertly, and without a mandate? Citizens, professional bodies, NHS employees, think and act tanks, and trade unions need to form a coalition to resist further privatisation and get the Health and Social Care Act repealed. 38 degrees is a powerful campaigning organisation. Use it to bring this about!

## the 21st century revolution

I believe most people have good intentions. However, I find it hard to say whether the perpetrators of these policies and actions are well-intentioned or not. At best, they must be out of touch with the mass of ordinary people and extremely unaware, especially of the adverse effects, particularly on the poor. One would think that, by now, the consequences should be evident to anyone with an open mind. Perhaps it is because, in the current political climate, leaders rarely feel able to admit mistakes.

***The need for strategic leadership.*** Political leaders, with their eye on the next election and newspaper headlines, do not provide the long-term strategies urgently needed. Their perspective is short. Many ministers are unqualified for their responsibilities and are appointed to placate factions in the party. Many are career politicians, uneducated in what is vital to perform their roles, without the experience or understanding of how to lead change. They may be talented but they got to where they are by being experts in politics. They do not provide the statesmanship required to lead a nation through the profound transformation needed to respond to the challenges of the 21$^{st}$ century: environmental, economic, social and technological, and the need to avoid violent conflict.

***Current economic policies are not working.*** We are part of nature and, like all other creatures, are interdependent and dependant on Mother Earth. Yet we are destroying it, squandering the Earth's capital as if it were income. I have argued that current economic policies, focussed on growth measured by GDP, are fuelling this crisis. Apart from ignoring the need for urgent action to address the causes of Climate Chaos, current policies are enriching the 0.01%

at the expense of the rest. They do not benefit the mass of humanity. They systematically transfer wealth from those who create it to the very rich. Imperialism was supposed to be over, yet we now realise the mass of us are colonised. The gap between rich and poor is growing; in Western countries, living standards for the majority are falling. We know that, in more equal societies, such as Denmark, there is greater wellbeing and happiness, and they are more prosperous – in more unequal societies, more talent is wasted. In the USA, the richest country in the world, there is huge poverty and the biggest gap between rich and poor. A 2013 UNICEF report ranked the US as having the second highest relative child poverty rates in the developed world. Unemployment levels are high.

**The Financial Crisis.** Excessive consumption, financed by debt and irresponsible casino banking, ultimately caused the financial crisis. Arguably, personal debt is a far more serious problem than public debt. Household debt in the UK now stands at £1.47 trillion, the highest ever figure, and 15 million Britons are going into debt just to cover their bills (Centre for Social Justice). However, unsurprisingly, given the underlying ideology, Osborne's focus is on public debt. The supposed need to cut public debt, through a policy of harsh austerity, is used as a justification for cutting the public sector. Business thrives on good public services and infrastructure paid for by taxation. Osborne's policy is making things worse for ordinary people, putting people out of work, thus reducing tax intake and increasing both public and personal debt. It bears down on the poor and harms the prospects of young people. Taxpayers are subsidising employers paying low wages. He has been consistently advised by bodies such as the Organisation

## the 21st century revolution

for Economic Co-operation and Development (OECD) to moderate his debt reduction targets, otherwise he will he will inflict hardship on the most vulnerable and jeopardise economic recovery.

Our money has been used to bail-out banks whose irresponsibility caused the crisis. We need to provide better incentives by making creditors more responsible for the consequences of their decisions. Austerity is inflicted on the poor, less severely on middle-classes, not the rich. Prices are rising whilst wages are falling. It is now recognised that a living wage is needed. Subsidies, largely hidden from the public, are supporting high carbon fuel and energy, nuclear power and unsustainable growth. Renewable energy would be increasingly affordable if subsidised to the same extent. Greening the economy, especially refurbishing the vast stock of leaky homes, would provide thousands of jobs. The business opportunities offered are being lost.

We are constantly misled by politicians, unwilling to admit their mistakes. Bluntly, they lie! The truth is this:

**Unnecessarily harsh and destructive cuts have prolonged the recession**, damaged the economy, damaged our society and delayed recovery. And we had 2 million people seeking jobs, and almost 1 million of those aged between 16 and 24. And because the fundamental flaws in the system are not understood and have not been addressed, a further crisis is likely to occur. We survived and thrived, despite the Government, not because of the policy measures it implemented. The UK Government's policy is based on Neoliberal ideology and free market capitalism

– not sound economic theory. Public sector, bad; private sector, good; cut taxes.

This truth should be told: the recession was caused by an international financial crisis, not New Labour, though they played their part by continuing Mrs Thatcher's policy of deregulation.

**We need to rethink the concept of globalisation.** Many of the UK's greatest companies have been taken over by foreign organisations without a stake in the wellbeing of our country, often for tax avoidance reasons. Food security is essential everywhere when food production everywhere is at risk because of climate change and turbulence. The creation of mega companies gives them too much power and undermines democracy. Under the guise of development, they undermine the production of food within poor countries and the development of economies that benefit them, not already wealthy nations.

**The pursuit of the cheapest source in a global market results in enormous hidden or "externalised" costs.** Cheap is expensive. We are losing economic sovereignty and security. Many of our best companies have been taken over by remote organisations with little interest in the wellbeing of our country. The creation of mega companies detached from local communities gives them too much power and undermines democracy. The lack of sufficient good work paying a living wage is putting a heavy burden on the state and hence the taxpayer. The loss of skills is damaging. Food security is essential when food production everywhere is at risk because of Climate Chaos. The global transportation involved contributes enormously to

### the 21st century revolution

Climate Chaos and global warming. Long sourcing chains are resulting in criminal adulteration of food. We need to prioritise local sourcing wherever possible to reduce our footprint.

***The UK economy is unbalanced***, too dependent on financial services, property development, speculation, and a few other sectors including arms production, not the best industry to be in. The armaments industry has a vested interest in conflict, war and military intervention. Dwight Eisenhower famously warned of the potential influence of the *"military–industrial complex"*. We should instead be investing in peace. There is relatively little manufacturing. Too much is concentrated in the South East where natural resources are stressed and housing increasingly unaffordable. We are virtually two countries: London and the rest, including a relatively impoverished North. Our economy is too dependent on and too much dominated by the vested interests of 20$^{th}$ century industries, oligopolies, particularly those based on fossil fuels.

***Banking and monetary reform are needed.*** Meanwhile, the banks and bankers have largely got away with it – though there have been substantial fines for miss-selling and other abuses. There have been no convictions of the reckless bankers who precipitated the financial crisis. Recently, George Osborne introduced a new offence – "reckless misconduct" – carrying a penalty of up to seven years imprisonment. But this is not the fundamental reform that is needed.

Inevitably, there will be further crises. Reform of the money system, the fundamental cause of high indebtedness, is not yet under consideration. Radical cultural change is needed. Banks should be there to serve; they do not. *"Casino"* banks and the *"boring"* banks, providing services to private and business customers, need to be completely separated. In the UK, there are five major banks. They are remote from their customers. There is not enough competition. It is similar to the situation with energy suppliers. We used to have many mutual building societies, designed to benefit members, without shareholders. Again, a few people have been greedy. And because the fundamental flaws in the system are not understood and have not been addressed, further crises are likely to occur. Proposals are provided in Chapter 7.

***The Greek crisis is a prime example of the "chains of debt"***, tying people to poverty and injustice that have been imposed on many developing nations in the 1980s and 90s, without democratic legitimacy, and now upon an ancient civilisation in Europe. I say this, irrespective of the outcome of the negotiations taking place as I write. The following is an edited version of literature provided by the Jubilee Debt Campaign.

### The Greek Crisis

The people of Greece, ground down by five years of Austerity, have not benefitted from bail-out loans from the IMF, EU and European Central Bank (the troika). It is the European and Greek banks that recklessly lent money to the Greek state in the first place. When the troika bailouts began in 2010, €310 billion had been lent to the Greek government by reckless banks and the wider European financial sector. Only 8% of this money

## the 21st century revolution

went to the people of Greece; the rest went to European and Greek financial institutions.

When the "troika" programme began in 2010, the Jubilee Debt Campaign warned that this was repeating mistakes made in developing countries. Bailing out European banks rather than making them cancel debts would ensure the private speculators would get repaid, whilst the public would pay the costs of having to cancel debts in the future. Austerity would crash the economy, increase poverty and unemployment, and increase the relative size of the debt. This is exactly what has happened.

This was also known within the institutions conducting the bail-out. Drawing on their own experience of failed bail-outs in the late 1990s and early 2000s, Argentina argued that a *"debt restructuring should have been on the table"*.

Syriza propose a debt conference based on the "London conference", which agreed debt cancellation for Germany in 1953. The 1953 conference agreed to cancel 50% of Germany's debt to governments, people and institutions *outside the country*, and the payments on the remainder were made, conditional on Germany earning the revenue from the rest of the world to pay the debt. Greece was one of the countries that took part in the debt cancellation. Syriza is proposing debt cancellation through a similar conference (some have suggested of around 50%), with the remainder of the debt to be paid over several decades to ensure that Greece can continue to repay. The German debt deal in 1953 was very successful. It supported German economic recovery and gave an incentive for creditors to trade so that they would be repaid.

The Greek and European debt crisis is the latest in a long line of debt crises that have affected all continents since bank lending was liberalised in the 1970s. The African and Latin American debt crises of the 1980s and 1990s were followed by the East Asian Financial Crisis of 1996-1998, the Russian default in 1998, and the Argentina default in 2001.

The current case in the US courts, where vulture funds forced Argentina to default on its debts, convinced developing countries that change is needed, and rules need to be introduced through the UN for resolving debt crises. In September 2014, a UN resolution was passed by 124 votes for to 11 against to establish a new legal framework for the debt restructuring process (such as a bankruptcy procedure for governments). However, despite the clear failures to resolve the debt crisis in Europe, the EU decided to abstain on the vote, with the UK and Germany amongst those who broke from this collective position and voted against. The current events in Greece and Argentina show it is clearly broken and in need of major reform.

A comment on Facebook says: *"This article provides much more relevant information about the Greek financial situation than anything I have read in mainstream, for*

> *profit publications."* (Thanks to Jubilee Debt Campaign – http://jubileedebt.org.uk)
>
> It needs to be added that the Greek economy is in urgent need of reform. The economy is unbalanced and tax evasion, under-reporting of income, special tax, pension and legal privileges for many professions and workers are widespread. Vested interests obstruct reform. Measures to strengthen transparency, competition and the rule of law are required. For more, see *Europe's fault line*, by George Magnus, *Prospect*, August 2015 (www.georgemagnus.com/greek-crisis-how-greece-became-europes-fault-line).
>
> Greece may be better off with its own currency (see Chapter 7).

Clearly, the UK is another example, though far less severe, with cruel effects for "ordinary" people. It also demonstrates what the people of the UK need to do to escape the chains of debt and austerity.

Proposals for Greece and general proposals for monetary reform and restructuring banking are given in Chapter 7: *An Economy that Works for All*.

**We need to change the way money is created.** The way our money is created is little understood. It is crucially important. It is a major cause of the current financial crisis and enormous public and personal debt indebtedness. Only 3% of our currency is created by the Mint. 97% of our money is created by commercial banks by issuing loans.

Banks have a vested interest in creating debt by lending, from which they make excessive profits. The result of the Government borrowing to fund infrastructure, schools and hospitals, instead of through taxation, is that it all costs more. The example of PFI has already been described. It was a way for Government to reduce taxation or hide how much it is spending.

**The effect on house prices.** Not surprisingly, the way money is created is also a major cause of rising property prices, not just the lack of house-building. Banks are incentivised to lend more and more money for mortgages and the Government is encouraging them to lend even more. It's never been so expensive to buy a home. In 1996, it took 17.5% of the average person's post-tax salary to pay for a mortgage; in 2013, 32.7%. House prices went up over 200% in the 10 years leading up to the financial crisis as lending into the housing market increased by 370%. Again, this made us poorer; the rich richer.

**Undemocratic management of the money supply.** The result of this system is that the commercial banks, not government, control the nation's money supply, a major aspect of national economic policy. This is undemocratic. In consequence, we are colonised and exploited by the banks. The system is a key part of how wealth is systematically transferred from those who create it to a wealthy minority.

There is a different way of creating money for both circulation and investment in public infrastructure, which I'll describe in Chapter 7.

### the 21st century revolution

***Incompetent governments driven by Neoliberal ideology are failing us*** when the whole world is in danger. It is all about short-term fixes, knee-jerk reactions to the media. Instead, we need solutions based on thorough research into what works, solutions that involve people on the ground. Far from fulfilling their promises of localism, it is government from the centre and interference from the top by noisy, opinionated politicians, unfit for the job.

***The public have lost confidence in many of our institutions*** – Parliament, banks, police, the NHS, the BBC, the media and the secret services. In recent years, there have been so many scandals, sex abuse by celebrities covered up for years, abuse by MPs and members of the House of Lords, incompetent organisations paid vast sums for projects that have not worked, whistle-blowers punished, prolonged and expensive inquiries often seen as white-washes. People are disgusted by the blatant greed of top bankers and business leaders continuing to pay themselves enormous sums whilst so many of the rest of us suffer. It is a sick society in which leaders appear greedy and self-seeking. Greed has affected the spirit of our nation. The idea that competent leaders and professionals need excessive financial incentives to do a good job runs counter to reality; it's a big turn-off to most people and sets a bad example. Most people are actually motivated by an inherent desire to do good.

Science, economics and business need to embrace ecology and morality.

There is no shortage of practical proposals to bring this about and I'll describe these in **Part Two**.

**bruce nixon**

## Further reading

A good source for Neoiberalism is Susan George – *A Short History of Neo-liberalism*
www.globalexchange.org/resources/econ101/neoliberalismhist

Wikipedia for Consumerism
en.wikipedia.org/wiki/Consumerism, http://en.wikipedia.org/wiki/Great_Society and en.wikipedia.org/wiki/The_Century_of_the_Self

# *Part Two*

## *Bringing about the revolution – it's already happening; we just need to give it a very strong push*

This part of the book offers a comprehensive response to the challenges described in the first part, all of which are inter-related. Some of the solutions are global; some apply specifically to the UK, though likely to be of universal relevance as all the issues are global. We have much to learn from each other about what works.

**We are at a stage in our history where the challenges we face are borderless.** If humanity is to survive, we have to give up short-sighted and competitive nationalist policies. Governments need to collaborate and work together; political parties need to do the same; we need to be internationalists. Prosperity needs to be redefined as the wellbeing of all. That is not yet the general mind-set of national leaders.

**bruce nixon**

We need a shared global vision. The United Nations is a forum within which this can be achieved. The European Union for all its difficulties is a pathfinder project. We in the UK need to put our own house in order and present a collaborative policy to the rest of the world, including our relationship with the EU.

We need a new social contract between the state and its citizens, comparable in ambition to that presented to the nation in 1945. Today, the challenges are very different and arguably much greater. Progressive thinking about political leadership has dramatically changed; the internet has provided a huge resource of free information and a means of making change happen; populations are less compliant. The nation needs to be inspired by a new vision for the early 21st century with policies to match.

# Chapter 6

## Environmental solutions – before it's too late

*"It's a strange kind of economic system that over-consumes natural resources, and yet leaves millions without jobs. A Green New Deal could address both points by putting people back to work, fixing the appalling energy and resource inefficiency of our infrastructure. If the financial system deems this impossible, then there is something wrong with the financial system."* **Tony Greenham, Director of Economy, Enterprise and Manufacturing, Royal Society of Arts.**

### Polly Higgins' UN Ecocide Law 5th Crime against Peace

I believe this is by far the most powerful solution as it would redirect and channel the energy of big corporations into serving society throughout the world.

Under current law, a CEO and their directors put the interests of shareholders first, that is money first. So any health and wellbeing provision for people and planet does not exist. Under current law, practices such as fracking, shale gas and coal bed methane processes, which all cause extensive damage and loss of ecosystems, cannot be stopped. As Polly Higgins says, *"Catch-me-if-you-can-fines have no legal teeth."* Fines for damage done now have little effect – they are a minor expense and compensation claims can be avoided over many decades, as in the case of the Bhopal disaster.

The Ecocide Law would create a primary legal duty of care as the *"superior responsibility"* of the directors of corporations. Ecocide would become an international crime, a law that overrides everything else.

The Rome Statute is the governing document that sets out the existing international Crimes against Peace. If we destroy the earth we walk on, we destroy our ability to live in peaceful enjoyment. For example, fracking, cumulatively, is an ecocide. Ecocide was included in earlier drafts until it was removed in 1996. You can read about the history of the law of Ecocide, which dates back to 1972, in The Human Rights Consortium research paper, called Ecocide is the Missing 5th Crime Against Peace ( http://eradicatingecocide.com).

The proposed amendment to the Rome Statute was submitted to the United Nations in March 2010. A full legal reasoning for a law of Ecocide and the definition was laid out – you can read what was submitted in Chapters 5 and 6 of Polly Higgins' first book, *Eradicating Ecocide*. She proposes as an amendment to the Rome Statute that Ecocide be legally defined as:

## the 21st century revolution

*"Extensive damage to, destruction of or loss of ecosystem(s) of a given territory, whether by human agency or by other causes, to such an extent that peaceful enjoyment by the inhabitants of that territory has been or will be severely diminished."*

Typical examples are the BP oil spill, as a result of which great damage was done in the Gulf of Mexico. More than 200 million gallons of crude oil was pumped into the Gulf of Mexico for a total of 87 days, making it the biggest oil spill in US history. 16,000 total miles of coastline have been affected; the protracted case of small farmers trying to force Chevron to pay damages for pollution in the Amazon rainforest; pollution caused by the Athabasca oil or tar sands, in Alberta, Canada; the unresolved threats to the Great Barrier Reef world heritage site in Australia from shale oil exploration and production along its coast. The good news is India's Supreme Court decision to reject Vedanta's proposed bauxite mine, backing India's 8,000-strong Dongria Kondh tribe, is a victory for tribal rights that could set a precedent for tribal people across the country.

By amending the Rome Statute, many countries can become signatories. There are currently 122 countries that are signatories to the Rome Statute. Any amendment to the Rome Statute requires the support of a two-thirds majority of the state parties (which now counts as 82 state parties).

Under this 5th crime, stewardship will become the number one priority – ownership secondary. Power will be vested in the UN to criminalise mass damage and destruction. It will establish a legally-binding primary duty of care to protect people and planet first. There will be a five-year transition from *"polluter pays"* to *"polluter doesn't pollute"*.

Ecocide law would also apply to governments supporting such practices and/or facilitating corporations committing such acts. There would be implications for the World Trade Organisation and the whole free trade mentality.

Companies, banks and governments will be responsible for restoring adversely impacted territories. If necessary, prosecutions will be pursued in the International Criminal Court (ICC).The starting point will be restoration. Where a member state is either unwilling or unable to act, ICC will step in. The first sentencing option is restorative justice; the hearing coming to agreement with parties adversely affected. Failing that, the law can be the enforced by a minimum two-years' imprisonment of the appropriate directors.

To support Polly Higgins' campaign, go to http://pollyhiggins.com/ and eradicatingecocide.com For an interview with her, see *Stir* magazine, April 2014 (stirtoaction.com).

## *Corporate charters*

To counter the abuse of power by transnational corporations, Rabbi Michael Lerner put forward proposals for corporate charters for companies beyond a certain size. The Tikkun community he founded proposes a Social Responsibility Amendment (SRA) to the US Constitution. The SRA will create a new system of Social Responsibility

## the 21st century revolution

Grand Juries (SRGJ), composed of 25 citizens, whose task would be to decide whether or not the corporation should be granted a new charter. He does not expect the amendment to be passed *"any time soon"* but it will stimulate the necessary debate about the principle.

*"A first step in developing that third path is to seek a New Bottom Line so that we judge institutions productive, efficient and rational, not only to the extent that they maximize wealth and power, but also to the extent that they maximize our capacities to be caring, ecologically aware, ethically and spiritually sensitive, and capable of responding to the universe with awe, wonder and radical amazement at the grandeur of creation."* **Rabbi Michael Lerner**

These proposals are further developed by the US National Constitution Center (blog.constitutioncenter.org/2011/10/a-constitutional-agenda-for-the-occupy-protesters).

Charters for corporations are not new. They were required for 100 years after the American Revolution. Legislators maintained tight control of the corporate chartering process. One of the most severe blows to citizen authority arose out of the 1886 Supreme Court case of *Santa Clara County v. Southern Pacific Railroad*. Though the court did not make a ruling on the question of *"corporate personhood"*, thanks to misleading notes of a clerk, the decision subsequently was used as precedent to hold that a corporation was a *"natural person"* not subject to state control (reclaimdemocracy.org/corporate-accountability-history-corporations-us/ and www.huffingtonpost.com/ralph-nader/corporate-charters_b_2759596.html).

**bruce nixon**

***The Responsibility of Boards to Stakeholders.*** The UK Companies Act 2006 Article 172 makes very clear that, in promoting the long-term interests of the company, the director(s) duty is to consider all relevant stakeholders, including customers, suppliers, employees, the community and the environment. There have been a few cases whereby representatives of these groups have tried suing a Board (e.g. Cadbury during the Kraft takeover) but, as I understand it, the Act does not adequately give much scope for suing a Board, even if it is clear that they are not properly exercising their responsibilities. It appears that Board Directors are narrowly interpreting their duties. The Act should be extended so that Company Boards are required to have specific representation on the Board from stakeholders other than shareholders: employees (as in Germany), community, customers, and be liable to criminal challenge in the courts on ethical and environmental failings.

Under S 171 of the Companies Act 2006, a director of a company must act in accordance with the company's constitution (very few companies write into their constitution that shareholders' interests/profit come second to other considerations. Whilst other considerations may be included, they are just that – considerations). S 172: 1) requires a director of a company to act in the way ... most likely to promote the success of the company for the benefit of its members as a whole ("members" being its shareholders first and foremost, then secondary to this is the director(s) duty to "have regard" for employees, community, environment, etc.).

## the 21st century revolution

The UK Companies Act 2006 introduced a statutory code of directors' general duties for the first time – before that, it was case law determined. The Companies Act 2006 was famously watered down last-minute by reducing the legal duty to prevent damage to the environment to a mere secondary "have regard". There are no enforcement mechanisms in the Act – this is a key failing and therefore allows companies to demonstrate "have regard" by, for instance, simply producing an annual report that includes a bit of greenwash.

The key failing is lack of enforcement: S 172 aims to align the best interests of the company with those of society as a whole, providing directors' to consider the interests of stakeholders when making decisions. However, **it fails to provide any method for stakeholders to hold directors accountable for breaching their duties. This is what must be changed**. (I am indebted to Polly Higgins for this information.) If you want to take action, go to Share Action – www.shareaction.org.

***Co-determination*** is a practice in which stakeholders such as employees play a part in managing a company, and they and representatives of the wider community have full representation on the boards of companies. The European Union drew up a Fifth Directive on Company Structure in 1974. The first co-determination (Mitbestimmung) laws began in Germany, providing worker participation in management. Worker representatives hold seats on the boards of companies employing over 500 people. In Sweden, 80% of the workforce is organised through trade unions, which have a right to elect two representatives to the board of all companies employing more than 25 people. This principle can be extended to include an elected community member in countries in which a company operates.

Where co-determination is practised, as in Germany, and employees are more involved, there are fewer strikes and days lost through illnesses, productivity is higher, pay higher, and conditions better, all leading to greater success. This has been known for decades. One might well ask: *Why it is not more widely practised?* The draft EU Directive on Company Law proposed a two-tier structure of a supervisory board and a management board. The supervisory board would be composed of one-third elected by shareholders, one-third by employees, and one-third independents co-opted by the other two-thirds. In 1977, Harold Wilson commissioned the Bullock Report, presenting co-determination proposals. But external events intervened, namely Mrs Thatcher. For the time being, a great opportunity was lost. We now have an even greater opportunity for the full and fair representation of all stakeholders, including the wider community, as described above. Nothing less than global international law is needed to impose a duty of care on corporations. Company law is needed to give substance to the term *"the triple bottom line: people, planet, profit"*.

*"The key is to provide for and empower the largest stakeholder of all – the community – to be equal participants in the decisions that affect the lives of those they represent."* **Polly Higgins**, *Eradicating Ecocide.*

# *The Green New Deal*

## the 21st century revolution

***Green New Deal Group's National Plan for the UK: From Austerity to the Green New Deal.*** This "National Plan" to detoxify the UK economy would end zero-hour contracts, remove hidden bank subsidies, cancel PFI, end tax avoidance and evasion, replace the current HS2 plan, and end the destructive "Dash for Gas". It would transform the UK economy to meet environmental and social challenges, create quality jobs in every constituency in the UK, end Austerity, and ignite a sense of shared national purpose. It would shift the nation from the politics of Austerity and rapidly-growing inequality to the age of the "Green New Deal".

It is designed to fundamentally transform a still-broken financial system and reduce the deficit, while transforming the UK's aging infrastructure to meet a range of environmental and social challenges.

***The Green New Deal*** requires initially a £50 billion-a-year programme to boost real economic activity, provide quality jobs on a living wage in every community in the UK, while reducing the UK's overall ecological impact. To begin with, this involves:

- ***A nationwide project to make every building in the country energy efficient*** and building hundreds of thousands of new, affordable, sustainably-sited, energy-efficient homes, creating jobs, affordable homes where they are needed most, and reducing fuel poverty.
- ***Realising the job creation potential in renewable energy*** – according to the Centre for Alternative Technology, the job creation potential of a zero carbon economy could be as high as 1.5 million new jobs

spread across the country, covering a range of skills and sectors of the economy – more than enough to provide quality employment for every person in the UK currently employed on a zero-hour contract.
- **Replacing plans for a HS2 rail link with a programme of improvements to the existing network**, particularly at pinch points, and the creation of new urban cycle networks in every town and city in the UK. Above all, the state needs to devolve powers to the regions and great cities to determine their own transport linkages. A prime example is the need for fast rail connections between the great Northern cities. This idea is now catching on.

The investment needed to implement the plan is not only readily available, but a carefully targeted programme would also help to reduce the UK's budget deficit. The programme would be funded by a range of measures, ending some of the worst financial abuses:

- **Tackling tax evasion and avoidance**. £70 billion in tax evasion and £25 billion in tax avoidance can and must be drastically reduced.
- **Investment.** Controls to ensure that banks that were bailed-out by the taxpayer also invest in the Green New Deal at low, sustainable rates of interest.
- **A form of "Green Quantitative Easing"** channelled directly into the transformation of the UK's energy, housing and transport infrastructure – very different from any previous round of QE, which have benefitted the finance sector and speculators, not the productive economy. Positive Money's proposals for Sovereign

Money, described fully in the next chapter, are similar (www.positivemoney.org/our-proposals).
- **Buying out costly PFI schemes** using Green Quantitative Easing, and using the money that would otherwise have been spent on interest payments to fund the Green New Deal.
- **Encouragement for pension funds and other institutional investors to support the Green New Deal.** These will earn a constant income stream, provide secure returns for pensioners and increase intergenerational solidarity.

For further information, go to the Green New Deal Group (www.greennewdealgroup.org/?page_id=200).

## *Creating Regenerative Cities*

Half the world population live in cities; half the world population are farmers living in villages. In his new book, *Creating Regenerative Cities*, and his article, *Our cities need regenerating; our villages must be valued*, in Resurgence & Ecologist, November, December 2014, Herbert Girardet emphasises the importance of both cities and villages to our wellbeing and survival. Whilst cities occupy 3-4% of the world's land surface, their ecological footprints cover much of the productive land and other resources on the planet. Small farmers feed more than half the world and are vital to our food future. Many are being driven off their land, ending up living in squalor in the outskirts of big cities. World food supply is threatened. Villages are equally important in countries like ours.

**bruce nixon**

London is amongst the most polluted cities in Europe, as argued in Chapter 3. Contrast this with Singapore, a city-state of 5.4m people, ranked among the top five countries on the 2014 Environmental Performance Index. Or Copenhagen, with its high levels of building efficiency, renewable energy, circular waste management, pedestrian streets, more cyclists than in most other cities and exemplary public transport, is working to become the world's first carbon-neutral capital city by 2025. Under independent Mayor George Ferguson, Bristol, with its many urban regeneration initiatives, will be the European Green Capital in 2015. There are many more examples all over the world, including Stuttgart, Nijmegen and Adelaide. Cities need to be regenerated so that they are healthy and sustainable places in which to live. 80% of Britons live in cities and we need to catch up with examples like these. We need to lobby mayors to follow such examples: www.worldfuturecouncil.org/fileadmin/user_upload/papers/WFC_Regenerative_Cities_web_final.pdf The Global Village Network (GEN) aids efforts to create sustainable villages all over the world (gen.ecovillage.org).

***District Energy in Cities.*** According to the UN, by 2050, two-thirds of us will live in cities. Cities account for 70% of global energy use and 40- 50% of greenhouse gases. Cities offer huge opportunities for climate resilient and affordable combinations of decentralised power, heating and cooling combined with energy efficiency measures that can save 58% of carbon dioxide emissions required by 2050 to keep global temperature rise within 2-3 degrees. UNEP's *District energy in cities* report (www.unep.org/energy/districtenergyincities), summarised in *Clean Slate* journal, Summer 2015, provides many examples. District energy is a core strategy in putting Paris on the pathway to a 75% reduction in CO2 emissions by 2050. In Copenhagen, Helsinki and Vilnius, nearly all the required heating is supplied through district networks. There are also synergies between production of and supply of heat, cooling, domestic hot water and electricity integrated with sanitation, sewage treatment, transport and waste. Examples from all over the world include Tokyo, Gothenburgh in Sweden, Anshan in China, Frankfurt Germany, Rotterdam in Netherlands, Dubai, Kuwait City, St Paul, USA, and Toronto, Canada. An added bonus is the employment such initiatives provide.

**Wellbeing in cities.** It is equally important to build wellbeing into cities and end isolation. In the UK, roughly 7.7m people live alone; loneliness is widespread and associated with ill-health. We are social creatures. Good design can enable happy mixed communities where people bump into each other, connect with their neighbours and support each other (*Building for Belonging: making our cities feel like home*, Kim Samuel in Resurgence Ecologist, May/June 2015). It is also important to provide space for growing food, either in back gardens or communal spaces, not only because of the likely global shortage of food, but also because of the contribution of growing things to wellbeing and mental health. Good examples of integrated urban environments include Bedzed in South London and Freiburg in Germany.

## *Zero Carbon Britain*

Power output from renewables is highly variable. So the Centre for Alternative Energy (CAT), in their publication, *Zero*

*Carbon Britain*, propose a comprehensive range of different sources and storage – a combination of wind, wave, tide, hydro, solar, solar PV, ground source heat and air source heat pumps, energy storage, biomass and waste reduction, and an updated grid for flexible distribution. One way of storing energy is in water, which can be pumped up, when the energy is not needed, and used to generate energy when required (Zero Carbon Britain zerocarbonbritain.org and zerocarbonbritain.com/images/pdfs/ZCBrtflo-res.pdf).

***Multiple Renewable Solutions – Sustainable Energy Networks.*** CAT's *Zero Carbon Britain* approach would be even more effective if implemented on a regional basis such as the North Sea or Europe. The European North Sea Energy Alliance (ENSEA) Scotland, Norway, Northern Germany and Northern Netherlands (ENSEA – www.ensea.biz) aims to develop a network to bring together energy know-how and research programmes through better coordination and exploitation of research. This was aimed to help achieve the European Union's 20.20.20 climate and energy goals to reduce greenhouse gas emissions by 20%; increase energy savings to 20%; and increase the consumption of renewable sources to 20%.

There can be similar networks all over the world.

***Energy storage.*** The National Grid says that, over the past 12 months, it made special payments of around £300m to energy companies to turn their power off to balance the system. How ridiculous. In March this year, the Government paid £8.7m to wind farms not to generate electricity. However, these problems will be solved as storage of energy in batteries improves. US AES, Northern Ireland's biggest power generator, plans to build a 100-megawatt battery facility that can store energy produced by wind farms. The company claims the facility will lower the cost to consumers, help meet renewable energy targets and improve the flexibility of the local grid. It says it could have the facility operational early in 2015.

## *Other global solutions*

**A Gaian League of Nations.** An important proposal is the formation of a Gaian League of Nations, set out in Ross Jackson's book, Occupy World Street – Towards a Gaian League of Nations.

The proposed Gaian League could be *"established and expanded by cooperation between top-down and bottom-up agents of change – a handful of small nations from the top and the grass roots of the world from the bottom."* A group of less than 10 small nations could take the leadership responsibility by formally founding the Gaian League as an alternative to the Empire, initially as a small prototype, but scalable. Once established, other nations would be invited to apply for membership. But this strategy *"can probably only succeed, in the face of Empire opposition, with massive support from civil society, not least from those within the Empire. This is the basic logic of the strategy."* Jackson speculates about the Nordic countries (possibly even the EU itself), Switzerland, New Zealand, Malaysia, Costa Rica, Venezuela, Bolivia, Sri Lanka, Bhutan, Maldives, Mauritius, Tunisia and Senegal. He goes further to suggest that, if the League becomes successful, *"it might well be tempting for bioregions or cultural regions of the larger states to consider seceding and joining the League in order to obtain for themselves the benefits of self-determination and cultural integrity. If so, this could be a major step toward a more stable and peaceful global society with a multitude of small states focused more on cooperation than on competition."* (Global Foresight Books – www.globalforesightbooks.org/Book-of-the-Month/ross-jackson-occupy-world-street.html)

**The Rebound Effect.** Mike Berners-Lee and Duncan Clark, in their book, *The Burning Question*, argue that as fast as improvements in efficiency are made and products and services become cheaper, they simply make way for vast increases in consumption and further emissions elsewhere. This comes partly from technological innovations that take up the savings in increased consumption. An example is whilst the efficiency of motor cars increases on the one hand, this is cancelled out by the production of larger vehicles, the constant desire for the latest model, and we may drive more. As energy reductions are achieved in Europe, there are increases in other countries. USA reduces its carbon footprint by developing solar energy and fracking, and then exports oil and coal to other countries in much the same way as UK exports its dirty industries. Population growth – this will tail off around mid-century – and the demand for Western levels of consumption and lifestyle are major factors too. Also things are not made to last, particularly clothing and shoes, and we are obsessed with the new, bombarded as we are with advertising on TV and whenever we use the internet. The authors conclude that there has to be a globally-agreed carbon cap.

## the 21st century revolution

***A Global Carbon Cap.*** This would have the beneficial effect on society of maximising the benefit to society of every unit of energy available. This is likely to be strongly resisted. Fossil fuel interests, oil, coal and gas, spend billions on campaign donations, influencing governments, misinforming the public, campaigning against regulations and building support in universities.

***Leave fossil fuels in the ground.*** Fossil fuel resources are running out. They are too harmful and what remains is too precious to be used. Their extraction is becoming too expensive and too damaging. This is another top solution. Mike Berners-Lee and Duncan Clark argue that we have to leave half the remaining fossil fuels in the ground. There is international agreement to limit global warming to 2°C, relative to the pre-industrial level. It has to be said that, almost certainly, this is an inadequate target. There have been many pledges, though not enough to achieve this target, but insufficient action. Emissions continue to rise exponentially, despite the growth of renewable energy and improvements in energy efficiency, mainly achieved in Europe.

This would have the beneficial effect on society of maximising the benefit to society of every unit of energy available. This is likely to be strongly resisted. Fossil fuel interests, oil, coal and gas, spend billions on campaign donations, influencing governments, misinforming the public, campaigning against regulations and building support in universities.

***Divestment.*** Now there is a growing call from cultural institutions, pension funds, universities and churches for disinvestment Already there are signs that fossil fuel is coming to be regarded as a poor investment. People are beginning to divest; not just for this reason but because it is a moral issue and a way of forcing the change we urgently need. And there are campaigns to divest as mentioned elsewhere.

**Carbon taxes.** Climatologist, James Hansen, Director of the NASA Goddard Institute of Space Studies, also recommends carbon taxes. He recommends a rising tax on fuels and redistributing 100% of the proceeds to taxpayers, known as *"tax and dividend"*, rather than backing the more widely used cap-and-trade approach, which has not proved effective. Carbon taxes would be phased-in, giving businesses and householders time to adapt.

The tax would be paid far *"upstream"*, i.e. at the point where fuels are extracted from the Earth or imported. Fuel suppliers and processors would pass along the cost of the tax to the extent that market conditions allow. Carbon included in manufactured products such as plastic, but not burned, will not be taxed. Carbon taxes will raise the price of carbon-intensive fuels and encourage low-carbon lifestyles.

Currently, the prices of petrol or diesel, electricity and fuels include none of the long-term costs associated with devastating climate change or the health costs of burning fossil fuels.

A direct tax on the carbon content of fossil fuels (coal, oil and natural gas) conveys crucial price signals that spur carbon-reducing investment. Taxing fuels according to their carbon content will provide incentives for both individuals and throughout every aspect of society, including new product design, capital investment and facilities location and government choices in regulatory policy, land use, taxation and *"enlightened"* subsidies.

The impact of added costs will be offset by distributing tax revenues to households *("dividends")* or reducing other taxes *("tax-shifting")*. Most carbon tax revenues will come from families of above-average means, corporations and government. The tax would be progressive because wealthier people use far more energy. They generally drive and fly more, have bigger houses, and buy more stuff. The carbon tax would be revenue-neutral to maximise the incentives to reduce emissions, while avoiding taxes that would drag down economic activity. Revenue-neutral means that little if any of the tax revenues would be retained by government. The vast majority of the revenues would be returned to the public, with, perhaps, a very small amount utilised to mitigate the disproportionate impacts of carbon taxes on low-income energy users.

Of course, this tax would be strongly resisted by the vested interests that finance our political leaders so we'll have a battle on our hands. But, as things get worse, we are going to win. And to be effective, it would require international collaboration.

Support for a carbon tax is growing among public officials, economists, scientists, policy makers, business people, environmental leaders and ordinary citizens.

**bruce nixon**

(Sources: World Watch Institute (www.worldwatch.org) and Carbon Tax Centre (www.carbontax.org).

---

## *The Steady State Economy*

As Kenneth Boulding pointed out (Chapter 3), we live on a finite planet. Yet we are already consuming 30% more resources than Mother Earth can sustain, and our consumption is continually rising.

### *We're taking far more than our fair share*

- We are consuming 130% (rising) of the Earth's bio-capacity, wasting it massively; 7bn of us now; estimated 9bn by 2050; demand for power to rise 53% by 2030 unless we become more efficient and waste less.
- Eco-footprints: Los Angeles rate = 5 planets; London = 3. Hectares per person: US 12.2; UK 6.29 (really double that because we rely heavily on imports); India 1.06. Safe and fair target 1.8 by 2050.
- Carbon footprints – $CO_2$ tonnes p.p. p.a. Qatar 44; US 17.2; UK 10 (double that because we have exported our dirty jobs); India 1.4; China 5.3; most African countries below 1.

- Safe 2050 target for planet, 2 tonnes per person = 90% reduction for us.

Consumption by rich nations is disproportionately high. It is crazy to advocate continuously increasing economic growth, as measured by Gross Domestic Product (GDP). We need to embrace the concept of a Steady State Economy because we live on a finite Earth. This is entirely possible. (See Buckmaster Fuller steadystate.org/meet/mission; Tim Jackson's book, *Prosperity without Growth: Economics for a Finite Planet* – www.theguardian.com/books/2010/jan/23/properity-without-growth-tim-jackson.)

**Contraction and Convergence.** Contraction and Convergence (C&C) is a proposed global framework for reducing greenhouse gas emissions to combat climate change. Conceived by the Global Commons Institute [GCI] in the early 1990s, the Contraction and Convergence strategy consists of reducing overall emissions of greenhouse gases to a safe level (contraction), resulting from every country bringing its emissions per capita to a level that is equal for all countries (convergence – www.gci.org.uk/contconv/cc.html). Rich nations' carbon footprints are far greater than those of poorer nations. So the proposal is that, through national carbon budgets, we would converge to equal per capita carbon footprints – a gradual transition to a safe level of two tonnes per person by 2050. That means a 90% reduction for us in the West.

**We need to rethink global trade.** To reduce emissions, we need to concentrate on exporting and importing commodities with the highest Foreign Exchange Earnings per Transport tonne (FEET index – www.treehugger.

com/cars/shipping-vs-airfreight-revisited-some-more-considerations.html).

## *So what can we do?*

At the end of their book, Mike Berners-Lee and Duncan Clark discuss our collective failure to tackle climate change and the lack of leadership. So we may feel there is nothing we can do. Doing something is better than doing nothing. We are a social species and we influence each other; individual actions can become a flood. (For instance, cycling has grown enormously in my hometown and all over London, thanks to a few souls braver than me.) They quote Bobby Kennedy's phrase, *"tiny ripples of hope"* will *"build a current which can sweep down the mightiest walls"*. Once again, we have to demand that our so-called leaders do the right thing – we are the majority and the vested interests are the few. Seven billion people are a powerful force. Support Avaaz and 38 degrees, petition and get on the streets again.

**A spiritual awakening.** In his article in Resurgence & Ecologist, September/October 2014, Samdhong Rinpoche, former Prime Minister of the Tibet government in exile, points out an even more fundamental change we need to make – a spiritual awakening, reconnecting business and morality. In the industrial age, we produce far more commodities than humans need:

*"Without encouraging human greed, no one would purchase all these mass-produced goods... The machine and the*

## the 21st century revolution

*market should be our servants. But in 'modern civilisation', the market has become our master."*

Also, there is constant innovation, regardless of need or purpose, to which we seem addicted.

All of us can play a part in this awakening, simply by the way we live and, for instance, by talking about it with friends and colleagues at work.

**_Imagine a different, simpler, happier way of life._** We need a new mind-set and new values. It would offer us enormous benefits. It is wellbeing that matters; wellbeing for us and all life on the planet. We know that having enough, not more and more stuff, brings us happiness. We know that, in fairer societies, people are happier and they are more prosperous. Most of us would be happier in a fairer world too. Simple things make for happiness: a loving family and friends, community, fulfilling work that makes a contribution to society, and having enough time with those we love. It would mean working fewer hours. It would mean travelling less and by different means – walking, cycling and in/round town buses. That would lead to better health, safer streets, more sense of community, less time stuck in traffic jams, less poisonous pollution and less stress. It would mean being more connected with nature, more often out in the countryside, woods, fields, downs and the sea – we know nature heals – and accepting we are part of nature and we cannot dominate it.

As I wrote earlier, it is now almost 22 years since the first United Nations Conference on Environment and Development was held in Rio de Janeiro in June 1992.

**ACTION**: It is essential that all of us do everything we can to make sure that firm, legally-binding commitments to action are finally made at COP21, the 21$^{st}$ Conference of Parties in Paris in December 2015. The need to prepare for a positive outcome is presented by the **Campaign against Climate Change** (www.campaigncc.org/COP-21Paris) and the **Green Alliance** (www.greenallianceblog.org.uk/2014/08/08/flaming-june-we-need-leadership-at-the-paris-climate-summit).

*Coalitions* like the Jubilee Debt Coalition (jubileedebt.org.uk) get results. **Avaaz** (www.avaaz.org/en) is a 34 million-strong community of global citizens. **38 Degrees** (www.38degrees.org.uk), with over 2.5 million supporters, works to bring about change in the UK. Also, use **Nation of Change (USA)** and **Global Justice Now** to petition.

*Dare to be great.* One citizen who dares to be great can make a huge difference. Polly Higgins decided to become the Earth's lawyer. Her inspiring little book, *I Dare You To Be Great* (pollyhiggins.com/books), helps me and it may help you. There are more campaigns in the **Resources** section at the end of the book.

# Chapter 7

## *An economy that works for all*

*The key questions are: What kind of world do we want? What kind of society do we want to live in? Then: What kind of economy is needed to provide it?*

### The Wellbeing Economy

We need economic policies whose goal is wellbeing for all human beings and all life on the planet. As I said earlier, we are part of nature and, like all other creatures, are dependent on Mother Earth. We are all interdependent; we are all one. Yet we are destroying our habitat and squandering Earth's capital as if it were income. Climate change is nearing a tipping point. And growing resource shortages, global injustices, inequality, self-interested foreign policies and military interventions contribute to terrorism. We run the risk of resource wars.

We need foreign policies that contribute to world wellbeing and peace. In the 21st century, we need collaboration rather than competition. We need a whole world outlook.

**bruce nixon**

We need to ask ourselves what makes life worthwhile. Arguably love, meaningful work, community, security and beauty in all its forms. At another time of change and uncertainty, William Morris said, *"Love and work, these two things only"*, and, *"The purpose of life is to employ one's talent to useful, beautiful and meaningful ends."*

We know that, in more equal societies, there is greater wellbeing and happiness and they are more prosperous. We need a strategy for a transition to balanced, green economy that offers good, well-paid work. The state's job is to facilitate a great transition into the industries of the 21$^{st}$ century and the research, education, skill development to match.

This chapter offers comprehensive policies for a sustainable, just economic system, whose focus is the wellbeing of all. Reform of the welfare state, banking, money creation, a basic income and the financing of infrastructure and affordable homes are key parts of this.

Sixty-seven years ago, in 1948, the UK Welfare State, based on the Beverage Report proposals (en.wikipedia.org/wiki/Beveridge_Report#cite_note-2), was implemented through a series of Acts of Parliament. It was widely popular and influential. Similar welfare schemes were created in Northern Europe and Nordic countries, including Germany, France, Denmark, Finland, Iceland, Norway and Sweden. But the world has changed since then and a bold, new approach is needed today. This is offered in the proposals of the New Economics Foundation (NEF) summarised here:

## the 21st century revolution

***Towards a New Social Settlement – People, power, planet*** – a framework for deciding how we live together, what we expect from our governments, and what we want to achieve for ourselves and others. It builds on the strengths of the post-war settlement, inspired by the Beveridge Plan, but moves on – because the world has changed profoundly – to offer a bold, new approach to the challenges we face today.

### Goals
The new social settlement has three goals:
- social justice
- environmental sustainability
- more equal distribution of power.

All three are intertwined and must be pursued together. They tackle severe contemporary problems:
- widening social inequalities
- accelerating threats to the natural environment
- accumulation of power by wealthy elites.

### Objectives
These goals lead to a set of objectives, which highlight crucial issues too often ignored in mainstream debate. Like the goals, they too are linked together and can be mutually reinforcing:
- Plan for prosperity without depending on economic growth.
- Shift investment and action upstream to prevent harm instead of just coping with the consequences.
- Value and strengthen the core economy of unpaid work, everyday wisdom and social connections on which all our lives depend.

- Foster solidarity, understanding just how much we depend on each other to achieve our goals.

This proposed settlement is part of NEF's work to build a new economy that serves the interests of people and the planet, not the other way around. We challenge the dominant view that the key to progress is to deregulate markets, promote choice and competition, and boost consumption. We offer a different set of ideas that promotes wellbeing for all within the limits of the natural environment, as well as more inclusive and collaborative ways of making decisions and working together. We aim to meet today's needs without compromising the ability of future generations to meet their needs.

To help realise our goals and objectives, we set out some proposals for practical change. They don't represent a comprehensive plan, but suggest a new direction of travel and a different set of priorities – our contribution to wider debates about what kind of society we want for the future.

### *Rebalance work and time:*
- a new industrial and labour market strategy to achieve high-quality and sustainable jobs for all, with a stronger role for employees in decision-making
- a gradual move towards shorter and more flexible hours of paid work for all, aiming for 30 hours as the new standard working week; an offensive against low pay to achieve decent hourly rates for all
- high-quality, affordable childcare for all who need it

# the 21st century revolution

***Release human resources:***
- support and encourage the unvalued and unpaid assets and activities that are found in everyday life beyond the formal economy
- adopt as standard the principles of co-production so that service users and providers work together to meet needs
- change the way public services are commissioned to focus on outcomes and co-production

***Strengthen social security:***
- turn the tide against markets and profit-seeking, developing instead more diverse, open, and collaborative public services
- build a more rounded, inclusive and democratic benefits system

***Plan for a sustainable future:***
- promote eco-social policies, such as active travel and retro-fitting homes, that help to achieve both social justice and environmental sustainability, and offset the socially regressive effects of carbon pricing and other pro-environmental policies
- ensure that public institutions lead by example
- establish ways of future-proofing policies

Written by: Anna Coote, with contributions from James Angel, Daniel Button, Jane Franklin, Eliane Glaser, Ian Gough, Sarah Lyall, Jacob Mohun Himmelweit and Julia Slay. (For report in full: www.neweconomics.org/publications/entry/people-planet-power-towards-a-new-social-settlement)

### bruce nixon

It is interesting to note that, based on the Office for National Statistics figures, there is a positive relationship between higher productivity and prosperity with a shorter working week (*Who works the longest hours in Europe?* – www.theguardian.com/news/datablog/2011/dec/08/europe-working-hours#data).

**Banking.** In recent times, UK banks have become more of a problem than an asset. Rather than serving the economy, through steady mergers they became out of touch with their customers and far too big a part of it, *"too big to fail"*, and a liability to the taxpayer. Their recklessness precipitated the financial crisis.

Germany provides a better model for banking. They have a different structure: national banks, regional banks and local banks charged with supporting local businesses. Small and medium enterprises (SMEs) provide the bulk of jobs, both here in UK and in Germany, and are the major source of innovation. The backbone of the German economy is its Mittelstand – a core of small and medium-sized firms; many have existed for generations and have proved their durability and resilience; some have grown large whilst retaining the same philosophy. Their most successful companies like BMW have constructive relationships with unions. Their leaders take pride in their businesses and take a long-term view. But in the UK, they don't get proper support from UK banks. In other countries, there are more credit unions. As ever, vested interests are obstructing the changes that need to be made. Germans tend to be unimpressed by our kind of capitalism.

## the 21st century revolution

The banks also took over the function of creating the nation's money supply.

**_Monetary Reform._** To deal with our environmental, economic and social problems, we need to reform the money system. The privilege of creating our money supply must be removed from commercial banks. Instead, it needs to be the role of the Bank of England or a similar public institution. The power to create money should only be used in the public interest, in a democratic, transparent and accountable way. The 1844 law made it illegal for anyone other than the Bank of England to create paper money. It should be updated and applied to the electronic money currently created by banks. When new money is created, it should be used to fund vital public services or provide finance to businesses, creating jobs where they're needed, instead of being used to push up house prices or speculate on the financial markets.

Public policy would then not only remove the compulsory debt now imposed on all citizens for using the public money supply. Public policy would become freer than now to encourage the use of democratically-controlled local and other complementary currencies; and it would also be freer than now to reduce today's systemic pressure to widen the growing financial gap between the majority of people and the comparatively few people able to share the unearned profits of the banks.

In 2010, the Government cancelled a programme to rebuild 715 schools because they'd run out of money. At the same time, the Bank of England created £375 billion of new money through a programme called Quantitative Easing.

Instead of this money being spent on something useful, it was pumped into the financial markets, benefitting the richest 5% but doing almost nothing to create jobs and stable economic recovery. It was a wasted opportunity.

***Sovereign Money.*** There is another way of creating money for investment in public infrastructure. Instead of using "Quantitative Easing" to support the banks, which they have used to bolster their reserves and not passed on to where it is needed, money can be supplied directly to pay for the infrastructure, schools, hospitals or housing projects hitherto financed by borrowing.

***Comprehensive reform of money, taxation and benefits.*** I asked James Robertson for his proposals. These are described fully in his book, *Future Money*. It can be freely downloaded as a PDF at www.jamesrobertson.com/futuremoney.htm.

Here is his summary:

1. ***The national money supply.*** Provide the national money supply as a public service. Stop the creation of money by commercial banks as profit-making debt and transfer responsibility to the central bank for creating money debt-free and giving it as public revenue to the elected government.
2. ***Taxation***
   (a) ***Shift taxes off "goods" and instead tax "harms".*** Reduce and eventually abolish taxes on value added, incomes and profits, which penalise useful work and enterprise.

## the 21st century revolution

(b) ***Develop other sources of revenue; shift taxes off "goods" onto "bads" or harms.***
Replace those with taxes or charges on things and activities that subtract value from common resources. These will include taxes or charges on rising land-rent values and on the use or right to use other common (mainly environmental) resources and take into account the capacity of the environment to absorb pollution and waste.

So the revenue from taxing fossil fuel production at source would be used to subsidise renewable energy and its development and energy saving measures for householders and compensate users for any rising costs. The proceeds of taxing food production known to be damaging to planet or human health, such as tobacco, sweet drinks and unhealthy food, would be used to subsidise fresh food, whole food, organic food. and foods known to promote health. These measures would both save lives, reduce ill-health and save NHS costs; they would provide extra funding for the nation's growing health crisis. Once again, prevention is better than cure. The charity, Sustain, says the UK consumes more than 5,727 million litres of sugary soft drinks a year. Adding a 20p tax for every litre sold would raise more than £1.1bn. A tax on sugar could raise billions. That would not only go a long way in helping meet the NHS funding crisis; it would help reduce the growing health problems caused by excessive consumption of sugar and reduce NHS costs.

3. ***Create a people-centred shift in public spending***
***Introduce a Citizen's Income*** – pay a tax-free income paid to every man, woman and child as a right of citizenship. The additional costs will be met by

eliminating or reducing government borrowing (and hence avoiding the costs of interest on government debt), ending perverse subsidies, savings by ending contracting out the provision of public infrastructure and services to the commercial business and financial sector, and further elimination of public sector inefficiency and waste.

***These are the potential benefits*** that most taxpayers and other citizens will benefit from:

1. ***Getting rid of the hidden tax*** that we all now pay to commercial banks every day as interest on all the bank account money in circulation.
2. ***Profiting from the one-off increase in public revenue*** resulting from the process of converting the money supply created by commercial banks as debt into money created free of debt by the Bank of England as an addition to public revenue for use, according to normal democratic budgetary procedures, either to reduce otherwise necessary taxes or to be spent into circulation on public purposes. The published national and bank statistics do not provide financial estimates of what those two benefits would amount to. But conservative assumptions of 5% annual interest payments and an existing total money supply of £1,500 billion to be replaced would provide:
   1. ***An annual total saving to all citizens of, say, £75 billion,*** and
   2. ***A one-off benefit to the public purse totaling some £1,500 billion*** over a three-year period of transition from the existing commercial-bank-

## the 21st century revolution

created money supply to the new debt-free money supply created to serve the public.

The hardships imposed by the continuing financial crisis on the majority of citizens who were not directly responsible for it, and the continuing public unrest resulting from them, bring an added sense of emergency to the overwhelming long-term arguments for monetary reform. (Thanks to James Robertson – jamesrobertson.com.)

**The Greek crisis.** James Robertson also addresses the Greek crisis. The Greek government could default, get out of the Euro, go back to the drachma and take away the creation of their money supply from the commercial banks (which Iceland is considering). Of course, they would have to do much more than that. It would mean reforming their economy. Greeks would have to kick the habit of not paying their taxes too. Greece would have to stop depending on loans from the IMF and ECB and instead finance their economy from within, as Japan does. Wealthy Greeks would need to invest in their own country, rather than putting money into property or other investments in other countries such as Germany. All kinds of abuses would have to stop. None of this would be popular with the 1% Greeks. But if it worked, it could be very popular with the mass of Greeks, especially the young. It may also be the route for Spain, Portugal and Italy.

James Robertson says:

*"These examples **and others** suggest that, sooner than we think, the world may accept the proposal to transfer the function of creating the whole of their national money*

supplies debt-free to public agencies serving the public interest. …. Public policy would then not only **remove the compulsory debt** now imposed on all citizens for using the public money supply. Public policy would become freer than now to **encourage the use of democratically controlled local and other complementary currencies**; and it would also be freer than now to **reduce today's systemic pressure to widen the growing financial gap** between the majority of people and the comparatively few people able to share in the unearned profits of the banks. … It's fairly obvious that reforming the money system at national level is a **necessary step toward a more decentralised money system as a whole**." (See www.jamesrobertson.com/news-apr15.htm.)

## Fair Taxation

"Fair Tax is the new fair trade… All it takes is for consumers, people who are taxpayers themselves, to back the companies that pay what they owe." **Ed Mayo**, Secretary General of Co-operatives UK

**Fair Tax** is an organisation that has established a **Fair Tax Mark** for organisations and is campaigning for a **Tax Dodging Bill.** Oxfam joined a coalition of organisations calling on all UK political parties to introduce a Tax Dodging Bill within 100 days of the UK May 2015 election that:
- Makes it harder for big companies to dodge UK taxes and ensure they're not getting unfair tax breaks
- Ensures UK tax rules don't encourage big companies to avoid tax in developing countries
- Makes the UK tax regime more transparent and tougher on tax dodging.

### the 21st century revolution

**Tobin Tax** The EU has been calling for a tax on international transactions, which would help stabilize financial markets and reduce short-term speculation, and the dangerous domination of the financial sector. Thus far, it has not had the support of UK government (en.wikipedia.org/wiki/Tobin_tax).

**Welfare Reform** The Tory government, from a Victorian Poor Law perspective, continues to expend a large amount of energy and resources trying to reform the welfare system. It makes negative assumptions about people, with much of the focus on abuse; it appears to be more about treating symptoms than tackling the underlying causes and modernising our economy.

It would have been far better to have put even more energy into creating an economy that provides prosperity for everyone, whilst preventing climate change and ecological destruction.

Universal Credit may be a good idea in principle. It requires a complex computer system that may be problematic to implement and possibly too rigid. The focus needs to be on creating a society in which everyone's potential is released, and impoverished, wasted lives become a thing of the past. If our economy is to have a future, this is essential. So mothers and families need much more support, including free or reasonably-priced, high-quality childcare and freedom from the extremes of poverty we are hearing about today.

A key function of the state is to help release the talent of all citizens starting from infancy. Diverse abilities are evenly spread amongst human beings, irrespective of their origins. An education system like ours is wasting a very large amount of that talent. So the focus needs to be on changing that from infancy upwards.

A Citizens Income could achieve the same ends as Universal Credit and much more.

*A Living Wage.* The Archbishop of York's Commission reckons a Living Wage could lift over a million people out of low pay by 2020 (www.archbishopofyork.org/articles.php/3109/living-wage-commission-reveals-blueprint-for-lifting-1m-out-of-low-pay).

---

### Our situation explained

- *A divided nation.* A great divide has opened up between the living standards and life chances of people in the different regions and the richest and poorest in our country. The gap in incomes, wealth and every other measure of wellbeing between both regions and socio-economic groups is wide and growing. The human costs, including ill-health and costs to the tax-payer, are very high and growing. The waste of human potential and damage to our future economic prospects is enormous. Many of our business leaders have paid themselves far too much, more and more every year, whilst the rest of us have faced declining real income. They have not taken responsibility for the corrosive effects of greed on their country. Unions are seen as enemies, rather than potential partners. All of us will suffer as a result.

- ***The 2015 election has created another big divide***: those who feel represented in the new government, and those who are not, and therefore feel frustrated and demoralised.
- ***Regional Investment.*** The regions need more powers. Recently, it was claimed that transport spending in London is £2,596 per head, yet only £5 in the North. (spatial-economics.blogspot.co.uk/2014/03/how-unbalanced-is-infrastructure.html).
- ***Gross domestic product per head***, a better guide to living standards than GDP, is still below the level in 2007. The rise in population from 61.8m to 63.7m reduced GDP per head by 3.1%. The cumulative rise in the Consumer Price index from 2008 to 2012 was 13.4%.
- ***Employment*** is up, close to 30m, but about 8m of these jobs are part-time. 5m are not working. 4.6 million are self-employed, equivalent to 15% of the workforce, compared with 13% in 2008, and 8.7% in 1975 (ONS). The growth in self-employment is reducing pay, job security and retirement income, and likely to reduce tax take too (TUC General Secretary Frances O'Grady).
- ***Numbers of people of retirement age are rising***, with the risk of widespread pensioner poverty and more and more stretched public finances. The state pension is one of the lowest in Europe.
- ***Excessive reliance on financial services and property development***, which are concentrated in the South East, drawing talent and investment away from other economic objectives. ***"Property Mania"*** is damaging London's sky-line, making housing

unaffordable, destroying communities, and the unique, often old, places of character that harbour diverse small businesses and creative enterprises. These are amongst the places that make London so attractive.
- **Manufacturing.** Continuing erosion of our manufacturing base adversely affects our balance of payments. Manufacturing can provide a better spread of quality, higher levels of skilled and well-paid jobs, and much-needed wider geographical spread of work. It can also make a greater contribution to exports and our balance of payments than services.
- **Investment.** The UK has one of the lowest investment rates in the world, ranking as low as 142 out of 154 countries as of 2012 (ONS). Our spending is disproportionate. In 2012, the UK consumed 87.8% of GDP, compared with the world average of 75.9% and developing countries 67.3% (IMF).
- **Productivity** per worker is low. The UK has lower productivity than USA, France, Germany, Spain and Italy, in that order, and the Euro area as a whole whilst working amongst the longest hours (OECD).
- **Skills.** Large numbers of people do not have the skills needed in the economy of now and the future. The creation of the right kinds of jobs and people with the skills to do them is vital. Education, re-education and skill development are keys to our future.
- **Squandering our assets.** Unlike Norway, we have not used our oil and gas assets to fund a sustainable future. We have allowed many of our assets, key sectors of our economy, research capabilities, great companies, investments and property to be sold off

to foreign buyers. We no longer have large, overseas investments bringing in income. Thus, we damage our future and live well beyond our means.
- **Short-termism.** We have used our assets to avoid facing our long-term decline, neglecting long-term investment for short-term gain. The focus of too many company directors and a banking system has been making money, rather than helping create wealth and wellbeing.
- **Household spending.** To achieve growth, we have relied too much on household spending (62% of GDP) and property. This results in increased borrowing, vulnerability to interest rate increases, rising house prices, growing inequality and, together with a housing shortage, difficulty for younger people wanting to rent or buy homes.
- **Homes.** In a decent society, everyone should have a decent home. If the economy is to prosper, the provision of sufficient, affordable homes is a top priority. As a result of decades of not building sufficient homes, particularly affordable homes, there is a serious housing crisis. This is particularly acute in London and the South East.

For much of the above, I am indebted to *There is an alternative – an economic strategy for 2015*, John Mills, published by CIVITAS.

***An inspiring alternative.*** Instead of focusing on National Debt, the deficit and continuing austerity, political leaders need to offer an inspiring vision for the future that will bring prosperity without growth to all.

**bruce nixon**

The fundamental need is to live lightly on the planet. The first question is what kind of society do we want? Then what economic policy and strategy is needed to achieve it? Assuming the purpose of the economy is *to create wellbeing for all, including all life on the planet on which we depend.* We need a whole focus on what makes for happiness and wellbeing – it's certainly not consumerism.

Here is a summary of proposals, about which there is considerable agreement amongst leading think tanks. Again, with considerable thanks to John Mills and others already mentioned or acknowledged below.

> ### A Sane Alternative
>
> - ***Top priority is to green the economy (as described in Chapter 6).*** A win/win: creating greater prosperity by greening the economy. Transfer subsidies from fossil fuels to renewables. Move away from weapons manufacture and trade, and instead use skilled resources for peaceful purposes and greening the economy. Act on the fact that we have exported much of our carbon footprint to poorer countries.
> - ***Prosperity without growth.*** This is a prosperity that does not continue to damage the environment, contribute to climate change and destroy our habitat. It means growth that enhances wellbeing whilst reducing our carbon and ecological footprints, and provides full employment and a Living Wage for everyone, backed up with a Citizen's Income.
> - ***Ending the North-South divide.*** There is now widespread support for devolving power to the regions, including tax-raising powers. Encouraging

## the 21st century revolution

highly-skilled manufacturing in the North will reduce unemployment in those regions, where it is highest, and benefit from a lower cost base than in the South East. It will help alleviate the chronic shortage of housing and high prices in the South. The good news is that companies in the North of England are growing at the fastest pace seen in any UK region, according to Ian Powell, Chairman of PricewaterhouseCoopers (PWC). There is cross-party support for George Osborne's *Northern Powerhouse* proposal to boost economic growth in the North of England, particularly in Liverpool, Manchester, Leeds and Sheffield.

- **City regions.** The concept of city regions with good infrastructure, transport links and more autonomy all over the United Kingdom is gaining traction. Recently the UK's 10 core cities met in London to launch their own "devolution declaration". These leaders, who run cities where almost 19 million people live, want a fundamental rethink of the UK constitution. The Core Cities Group (www.corecities.com) – Birmingham, Bristol, Cardiff, Glasgow, Leeds, Liverpool, Manchester, Newcastle, Nottingham and Sheffield – are demanding a *"radical modernisation of our centralised state"*. City-based regions will have more power to raise money and spend it; more power over planning, transport, homes, schools and health. To his credit, George Osborne supports this initiative. But The Campaign for Better Transport say that the Powerhouse plans are at risk of derailment, with massive electrification projects put on hold. They are urging him to commit to pausing road spending, not rail upgrades.

- ***Oxford 2065*** as mentioned earlier, provides a visionary picture of what an integrated, sustainable city region could look like in 2065, including ways of meeting the growing needs for educational and office buildings, integrated transport, food production, energy and power, student accommodation, homes and open spaces. It aims to be an exemplar for Europe. See two articles in *Oxford Today*: *Oxford 2065* and *Sustainability is the real bottom line* (issuu.com/oxfordalumni/docs/oxford_today_trinity_2015-digital?e=4233363/12371376).
- ***Rebalancing the economy towards exports***, substituting home production, would also correct our balance of payments deficit. This is obviously a win-win with the benefits to employment.
- ***Vocational Education.*** More is needed for 15-18-year-olds. UK: 32% taking vocational courses; 21% youth unemployment. Netherlands: 67% and 10% respectively.
- ***High levels of employment*** at higher levels of pay will reduce both poverty and inequality. There is no shortage of work to be done in transforming our economy and society and making it more sustainable, happier and healthier. And it does not involve increasing our footprint on the planet – on the contrary. A minimum wage of £10 is proposed, with higher minimums in the London region and the big regional cities.
- ***Homes.*** Sufficient, affordable homes are essential to wellbeing and a thriving economy. The Government needs to build 250,000 new, affordable homes annually to prevent a predicted 750,000 housing

shortage by 2025. These need to provide the sort of communities that we know human beings thrive in. They need to be beautiful, not devoid of nature. We know that trees and open spaces are essential to human health. Developments should include the necessary infrastructure for sustainable communities – sustainable transport, cycle lanes, school places, surgeries, shops, public open space, provision for growing vegetables and fruit, and meeting places – and incorporate modern building methods, such as factory-built; the norm in many northern European countries. An ambitious strategy for refurbishing rather than demolishing older homes is needed. Amongst the wealth of proposals are *Together at home: A new strategy for housing*, proposed by IPPR. See also *Britain's housing crisis is a human disaster. Here are 10 ways to solve it*, by Rowan Moore, *The Guardian*, Saturday, 14th March 2015, and Homes for Britain Campaign in **Resources** at the end of the book. Examples of sustainable housing communities are Bedzed in South London, Hockerton in Northamptonshire and Vauban in Freiburg, Germany.

- **Affordable or free high-quality childcare** is vital for mothers and the early development of children. It is far better provided in other countries.
- **Shorter working hours**, coupled with greater investment, as practised in Belgium, the Netherlands and Germany can produce higher creativity, innovation and productivity, and lead to a better distribution of work – some people have too much, work too long; others are work-poor. The New Economics Foundation gives 10 good reasons for

a shorter working week (www.neweconomics.org/blog/entry/10-reasons-for-a-shorter-working-week).
- **Manufacturing.** As part of creating a balanced economy and reducing our dependency on financial services, the scale and competitiveness of manufacturing – it has to be a new kind of manufacturing – needs to be increased. Manufacturing needs to be about 15% of GDP, as opposed to the current 10%. Otherwise, we will never get our balance of payments, and hence the Government deficit, under control. This will require increased investment in research and development, better technical education, training and retraining. An increase in UK manufacturing output would inevitably involve some new products and processes but a good deal of it being production of existing products, which would not in future have to be transported halfway across the world from the Pacific Rim (John Mills).
- **Constructive partnership between employers and trade unions.** We need to see trade unions as key partners, providing a constructive way of involving employees in creating success, as is done in Germany. Certainly, unions abused their power in the past. But weak employee representation resulting in low pay and poor employment conditions is not in the society's interests.
- **Increase investment.** Too much is invested in making money from money, speculation, rather than creating wealth. Gross investment as a proportion of GDP needs to increase from the current 14% to well over 20% (John Mills).

- **Public services and investment** will be more affordable in a healthy economy but, as argued above, investment in infrastructure can be financed by Sovereign Money, instead of creating costly debt.
- **Radical reform of the banking and money systems**, described above, is needed to enable many of these changes to happen. To prevent another financial crisis, investment banking and banking services should be completely separated. The power to create money for profit, which incentivises the creation of debt, should be taken away and become the responsibility of an independent public service. Regional and local bank services and a fully-funded Green Investment bank should be set up.
- **Taxation.** Comprehensive proposals were described earlier in this chapter, including James Robertson's, Oxfam's and Fair Tax's campaign for a Tax Dodging Bill, a Fair Tax Mark and a Tobin Tax.
- **A strengthened UK Companies Act** (as proposed in Chapter 6) that reinforces directors' duty to consider all relevant stakeholders including customers, suppliers, employees, the community, the environment and future generations.
- **Responsible Purchasing Act.** Lastly, governments have huge opportunities to use their purchasing power to deliver social and environmental benefits, both within their countries and internationally, and in that way, influence its suppliers. In the UK, CORE is campaigning for a Responsible Purchasing Act (www.ethicalconsumer.org/aboutus/ourmission/ourmanifesto.aspx).

bruce nixon

***Zero Marginal Cost Society.*** Jeremy Rifkin's book, *The Zero Marginal Cost Society: The Internet of Things, the Collaborative Commons, and the Eclipse of Capitalism*, describes how an internet-facilitated *Internet of things* could enable a shift from markets to collaborative commons, and large increases in productivity with costs close to zero. It could also lead to immense power in the hands of very few people, further polarisation between the very rich few, and the rest of us, depending on how we use such technological innovations. (For a review of his book, see www.theguardian.com/commentisfree/2014/mar/31/capitalism-age-of-free-internet-of-things-economic-shift.)

## *So what can we do?*

***ACTION: To be part of this revolution***, decide which of these organisations to join and work with. There is no shortage of practical proposals – CIVITAS, Compass, Ethical Consumer, Institute for Public Policy Research (IPPR), James Robertson's *A Sane Alternative*, New Economics Foundation (NEF), Nation of Change in USA, The People's Assembly, Positive Money/Sovereign Money, Resolution, Sutton Trust and Rowntree Foundation, Rethinking Economics and your nearest Transition town. Use Avaaz, 38 Degrees and the global 350 Degrees. There are similar organisations all over the world – see **Resources** at the end of this book.

# Chapter 8

## Resolving conflict without violence – Learning to rejoice in difference; ending violent conflict and war

> "We have to remember that, only a few hundred years ago, we (in the UK) were busy putting heads on spikes, butchering women and children in the name of religion, burning people at the stake, and more. It took us decades, centuries, to escape from brutal forms of feudalism; the Arab Spring began only three years ago." **Dr Scilla Elworthy**, Founder, Oxford Research Group and Peace Direct, Councillor of the World Future Council

**Violence takes many forms.** We need to give all of them up. There is violence to animals in factory farming, violence towards women and children, violence to aboriginal people when their lands are destroyed by deforestation or mining, and violence to Mother Earth. Driving is often violent: worldwide, driving results in as many deaths and injuries as conflict and war (of course, bad roads play a major part in poorer countries). Words are violent when they abuse or put someone down; this is a daily occurrence in the House of Commons and the news. Listening with respect is the way to learn and reach lasting solutions that take account of everyone's needs and concerns, and prevent or resolve conflicts. By listening, we often change our view.

Fortunately, the predominant human energy is love, not hate. That is to be seen in every aspect of daily life wherever one goes.

Satish Kumar, in his article, *The Path of Peace* in *Red Pepper*, June/July 2014, speaks of...

## *The principle of doing no harm*

He says that anger is violence to oneself. Anger is punishing oneself for the mistakes of others; anxiety, inferiority complexes and cynicism are also violence to oneself. There is social and political violence in the form of colonialism, racism, exploitation of the weak, poverty, social injustice, sexism and all kinds of discrimination. The pursuit of a just and equitable society is integral to the principle of non-violence. As quoted earlier in Chapter 2:

*"No one is born hating another person because of the colour of his skin, or his background, or his religion. People must learn to hate, and if they can learn to hate, they can be taught to love, for love comes more naturally to the human heart than its opposite."* **Nelson Mandela**

**Life is sacred.** That is the teaching of all religions. Nothing is worse for a mother and father, for a family, than to lose that child they nurtured so lovingly, at any stage in life, and particularly in war. In a civilised world, war is a crime against humanity. Violence in civil society leads to prison – why not in the case of initiating military killing not agreed by Parliament under the auspices of the UN?

Imagine if it were not Bagdad but London – or any Western city – that had suffered an onslaught of missile destruction and thousands of us fled our homes to the remote regions of our islands or other countries and ended up in refugee camps.

More than 3 million have fled the war in Syria, and 6.5 million are displaced within Syria; more than half of those uprooted are children (UN). We know the effects on children are traumatic. Now the World is horrified by the rising toll of tragic drownings in the Mediterranean and Europe faces a crisis as the numbers of migrants soar.

Samdhong Rinpoche, quoted earlier, says:

*"Co-operation is the way to reduce violence. Conflict is the way to increase violence."*

**Surely it is time for humanity to give up violence as a means of resolving conflict.** This must be the lesson of the Western interventions in the Middle East and North Africa and the wars of earlier generations. WW1, *"The war to end war"*, followed by the *"Peace to end peace"*, led to WW2. These conflicts have their roots deep in history, in flawed foreign policies that put self-interest ahead of fairness and world peace. Military action should only be initiated in exceptional circumstances, and with the authorisation of the UN.

**bruce nixon**

Surely we have learned that we rarely end violence with violence. War almost always results in more war. World War One and its aftermath created the conditions for World War Two.

In his editorial in Resurgence & Ecologist, September/October 2014, **Satish Kumar** wrote:

*"While ordinary people around the world hunger for peace, political and military leaders and the arms trades seem to have an unshakable faith that it is wars that will bring peace. They ignore the long history of their failures and continue to prepare for wars in the name of 'national interest', 'homeland security' and 'territorial integrity'. But all these goals remain elusive. ...The 21$^{st}$ September is the United Nations Day of Peace, celebrated around the globe. This day reminds us of the simple and self-evident truth that war and violence are futile... The optimist in me would like to think that wars and conflicts may be a thing of the past."*

**Water and Peace.** In his article, *Blue Peace*, published in *Inspires*, the Magazine for Oxford Politics and International Relations Alumni, 2014, Sundeep Waslekar argues for a global centre to facilitate active water co-operation between countries to prevent war. He cites many examples of this already happening. He believes water is at the core of life-systems and a decision to co-operate in this sector has implications for electricity, agriculture, urbanisation, livelihood, migration and political stability. He has facilitated dialogues between Western and Islamic leaders, hosted by the Strategic Foresight Group (www.strategicforesight.com), in collaboration with the Alliance of Liberals and

### the 21st century revolution

Democrats in the European Parliament and the League of Arab States (en.wikipedia.org/wiki/Sundeep_Waslekar).

**Valuable lessons** are contained in *Wars in Peace*, by Professor Malcolm Chambers, Research Director and Director (UK Defence Policy) at Royal United Services Institute (RUSI), analysing the success and failure of Britain's military operations since the end of the Cold War. In compiling the following summary, I thank Oliver Wright for his report Costly failures: Wars in Iraq and Afghanistan cost UK taxpayers £30bn, Independent, 27th May, 2014 http://www.independent.co.uk/news/uk/politics/costly-failures-wars-in-iraq-and-afghanistan-cost-uk-taxpayers-30bn-9442640.html

**Britain's support of US interventions** in Iraq and Afghanistan cost the UK almost £30bn – or £1,000 for every taxpayer in the country. £30bn would pay for: 1,464,000 more NHS nurses or 408,000 NHS consultants. This is nothing compared with all the lives lost, severe injuries, traumatic effects on children and damaged lives.

The interventions in Iraq and Afghanistan are to be judged as *"strategic failures"*. *"There is no longer any serious disagreement"* that Britain's role in the Iraq War served to channel and increase the radicalisation of young Muslims in the UK. It is estimated that 100,000 Iraqis were killed and two million refugees fled to neighbouring countries. Failed interventions in Iraq from 2003, and Afghanistan after 2005, account for 84% of the total cost of British military interventions since 1990.

### bruce nixon

While earlier interventions in Bosnia, Sierra Leone and Iraq in 1991 could be broadly described as successful, the case for later interventions is much less clear-cut. It suggests British aims in Afghanistan could have been met by a far smaller, more strategically-focussed force.

Policy makers on both sides of the Atlantic misjudged the ability of military might and money to effect change in countries with no history of democracy.

*"The underlying flaw in both of these operations was that US and UK leaders thought that their superior military power, along with large amounts of money, could shift foreign societies onto quite different paths of political development... The most important conclusion, however, may be that, in the end, their contribution to change was much lower than that resulting from other factors, most of which have proven remarkably resistant to shaping by outside powers."* **Oliver Wright**

Professor Malcolm Chalmers concludes that the UK's most successful interventions were those with *"clear but limited strategic objectives"*. Attempts at nation-building in Afghanistan and counter-narcotic operations were particularly ineffectual.

*"The intervention in southern Afghanistan did not succeed in reducing opium production in Helmand – one of the main reasons the UK chose to focus its efforts on what is an otherwise relatively unimportant province in economic or strategic terms. Afghanistan remains the world's leading producer and cultivator of opium and cultivation in Helmand is higher today than it was before the British arrived."*

### the 21st century revolution

He concludes the US-led invasion caused many more civilian deaths than would have been the case if Saddam had remained in power.

*"While leaving Saddam in power would have involved other costs in terms of human development and human security, these would probably not have led to casualties on the scale of the civil war that followed the invasion.*

*Saddam was one of the most brutal dictators of the late 20$^{th}$ century. [But] by 2003, the scale of these misdeeds had been much reduced, not least because of the containment measures put in place after 1991."*

However, in his foreword to the book, General Sir David Richards, former Chief of the Defence Staff, suggests any failures in Iraq and Afghanistan should not be used as an argument not to use force again in the future.

*"History is clear. There will sometimes be no alternative to standing up for oneself, for one's friends or for what is right. Too many people, the intelligentsia to the fore, are in denial of this inevitability."*

The total bill does not include the cost of the withdrawal from Afghanistan; nor the displacement of some four million people, the cost to families who have lost their loved ones or parents, nor the traumatic effects on members of the armed forces suffering from post-traumatic distress.

We hear of soldiers sacrificing their lives for their country. But in fact, most often, they die for reckless political leaders, most of whom have no first-hand experience of war or the consequences for civilians, and do not calculate the disastrous outcomes of their interventions. The chaos unfolding now in Iraq and Syria, especially the barbaric atrocities committed by the Islamic State, formerly known as ISIS, should be enough to convince us that war should only be embarked upon in the most extreme circumstances, such as the Nazi threat to civilisation.

## *Our efforts should be concentrated on prevention and conflict resolution*

*"If you want to make peace with your enemy, you have to work with your enemy. Then he becomes your partner."*
**Nelson Mandela**

Working with powers in a region where there is conflict is likely to be more productive. Building up armaments and alliances is likely to be seen as a threat. The arms race between Britain and Germany, for which Britain was arguably responsible, may have been a factor in causing the Great War. This probably partly explains the behaviour of Vladimir Putin over the Crimea.

**Trident.** Our political leaders argue that we need Trident and our nuclear weapons to maintain our position in the world. Simon Jenkins, in his article, *The case for Trident is absurd. Scotland may help us get rid of it*, says, *"Prestige, not defence, is the only reason to keep this £100bn albatross."* The Campaign for Nuclear Disarmament (CND) (www.cnduk.org) says, *"... the time has come to end notions of status based on how many people you can kill – and the ability to exert power of life and death over others."* Whatever the

## the 21st century revolution

costs of buying and operating a successor to Trident may be – estimated at around £70bn plus £30bn to keep the existing warheads in service until 2023 – it is a lot of money, which CND argue could instead boost high technology engineering jobs in sustainable industries or pay for social needs, not weapons of war.

Furthermore, we should get out of the arms trade and transition these industries to better purposes such as the weapons of peace and sustainability. Campaign Against the Arms Trade (CAAT).

**ISIS.** In his article in *Project Syndicate*, Mohammed bin Rashid Al Maktoum, Vice President and Prime Minister of the United Arab Emirates and Ruler of Dubai, says:

*"If we are to prevent ISIS from teaching us this lesson the hard way, we must acknowledge that we cannot extinguish the fires of fanaticism by force alone. The world must unite behind a holistic drive to discredit the ideology that gives extremists their power, and to restore hope and dignity to those whom they would recruit. ISIS certainly can – and will – be defeated militarily by the international coalition that is now assembling, and which the UAE is actively supporting. But military containment is only a partial solution. Lasting peace requires three other ingredients: winning the battle of ideas; upgrading weak governance; and supporting grassroots human development."* (www.project-syndicate.org/commentary/mohammed-bin-rashid-al-maktoum-calls-for-a-broad-development-agenda-to-defeat-the-middle-east-s-ideologies-of-hate)

**bruce nixon**

*In time, war will be abandoned*, I believe, though it could take several hundred years. For this to happen more rapidly, sufficient of seven billion people need bring pressure to bear and create a tipping point. This has to start with us in the West; we have to take responsibility for ourselves. A World War Three could emerge from the competitive conflict we are witnessing today; it could be a war between nations but it could also develop from breakdowns of law and order within nations (James Robertson's Newsletter, August 2014).

UN Secretary-General, Ban Ki-moon, has urged world leaders to address emerging crises before they become bigger and costlier for all. He said the United Nations needs to re-examine and refine its approach to preventing conflicts. One of his core priorities is to improve the organisation's ability to act early and act preventively. It's time for a new era of collaboration, cooperation and action from the Security Council:

*"When Member States join forces, we can achieve much. This Council's consensus on removing chemical weapons from Syria is one recent case in point. Even modest United Nations actions can have an important impact when we have the Security Council's united support – speaking with one voice – for early engagement. However, when there is limited consensus – when our actions come late and address only the lowest common denominator – the consequences can be measured in terrible loss of life, grave human suffering and tremendous loss of credibility for this Council and our institution."* **Ban Ki-moon**, 21st August 2014 (www.unmultimedia.org).

## the 21st century revolution

The UN High Commissioner for Human Rights, Navi Pillay, has said the Security Council too often lacks resolve to end conflicts and save lives. In her final report, she criticised the body for its ineffectiveness on Syria and other intractable conflicts, saying members have often put national interests ahead of stopping mass atrocities.

*"I firmly believe that greater responsiveness by this Council would have saved hundreds of thousands of lives. Syria's conflict is metastasizing outwards in an uncontrollable process whose eventual limits we cannot predict."*

Referring to conflicts in Afghanistan, the Central African Republic, Congo, Iraq, Libya, Mali, Somalia, South Sudan, Sudan, Ukraine and Gaza, she said:

*"These crises hammer home the full cost of the international community's failure to prevent conflict. None of these crises erupted without warning."* (www.theguardian.com/world/2014/aug/22/un-human-rights-chief-criticises-security-council-over-global-conflicts)

Nelson Mandela finally achieved equal rights for black Africans by working with his former enemy, F. W. de Klerk. Abraham Lincoln ended slavery in the USA by mastering how to work with his adversaries. It is also said that, to achieve progress, it is essential to understand the mind-set of your adversary, however distasteful it may be.

We in the West need to put an end to violent interventions and war. Surely that is the lesson of Western interventions in the Middle East. We need idealists and statesmen; people who, rather than blame the other party, accept responsibility, work with them and seek win-win solutions.

## *Foreign policy and peace – we need international collaboration*

Humanity collectively faces the greatest crisis in its history. Instead of foreign policies based on self-interest and competition for resources, we need international collaboration to solve these problems.

Once again, the solutions exist; all over the world, there are innumerable examples of success in preventing violent conflict. It is ignorance of these approaches and the mind-set that needs to be changed particularly in our political leaders. We need to accept the simple lesson that violence in any form is inexcusable and utterly irresponsible in any aspect of human life. It simply does not work.

As A H Bodkin, KC, said in May 1916:

*"War will become impossible if all Men* (that includes women) *were to have the view that war is wrong."*

During the Great War, Bertrand Russell, E. D. Morel, both of whom were imprisoned for six months, Emily Hobhouse, Fenner Brockway, who was imprisoned and spent eight months in solitary confinement, Keir Hardy and Sylvia Pankhurst all tried to stop the war. In 1916, Emily Hobhouse travelled to see the German Foreign Minister, whom she had known before the war, to seek possible peace terms. She brought back a possible basis but the British Cabinet

## the 21st century revolution

Ministers refused to see her, regarding her as a crackpot. 20,000 men refused to go into the army, of whom 6,000 went to prison. They were the pioneers. Today, the anti-war movement is much stronger (thanks to the same issue of *Red Pepper*, quoted above).

Since then, things have changed dramatically. Two million of us marched in London, and many more all over the world, to prevent the Iraq War, although Tony Blair was not deterred. Governments are more reluctant to get involved in military action, and lack the necessary public support, since the failures of that war and the intervention in Afghanistan. Working with our *"enemies"* to understand their mind-set and bring about reconciliation, as Lincoln did to end slavery in the USA, and Mandela and Tutu did in South Africa, to bring about justice for black people, is required. Ultimately, it will have to be the way forward in the Middle East and the Ukraine.

**Our best hope is to completely change the mind-set that supports war.** Like David Aldridge, author of *How ought war to be remembered in schools?*, who says we need to rethink our approach to Remembrance Day, I have reservations about it. I think we need to focus the day on how we can prevent war, as well as remembering and giving support to those who are suffering and the bereaved as a result of war, including all the innocent civilians and children.

**Road peace and violence.** Finally, there is one form of violence that is largely overlooked. The World Health Organisation (WHO) estimates that deaths on roads are 1.275 million annually. WHO also estimates that, for every person killed on our roads, another four suffer lifelong disabilities. These figures are probably higher than those involved in violent conflicts and war, and they will increase rapidly with the sales of motor vehicles. Road crashes in poorer countries, where the numbers are far greater, are mainly due to poor infrastructure, but inexperience and attitudes also play a part. If we add the other deaths and disabilities caused by motor vehicles, most notably traffic-generated air pollution, motor vehicles would be one of the leading causes of death. Here again, we need a transformation in our attitudes, especially towards driving.

## *So what can we do?*

***ACTION:** If you want to work for peace and end violence*, decide which of these organisations you would like to support actively: Campaign Against Arms Trade, Campaign for Nuclear Disarmament (CND), Institute for Economics and Peace (IEP), International Campaign to Abolish Nuclear Weapons, Oxford Research Group, Peace Direct, Responding to Conflict (RTC), Women's International League for Peace and Freedom (WILPF), Wool Against Weapons, and Road Peace for peace and justice on the roads.

# Chapter 9

## Transforming democracy – a great power shift from politicians to people

### We need a bold new vision of democracy, fit for the 21st century

*"We are 21st century citizens, doing our best to interact with 19th century-designed institutions that are based on an information technology of the 15th century... which has no dialogue capacity. It's time we start asking: What is democracy for in the internet era?"* **Pia Mancini**, DemocracyOS at TED Global 2014

Pia Mancini is one of the founders of the Net Party, a political party, headquartered in Argentina. She is also a co-founder of DemocracyOS, a free source to help give more weight to the opinions of citizens (direct democracy). Her political goal is to make a *"democracy of the 21st century"* that would result in greater impact of citizens in politics, notably through new technologies, with the internet as the main element.

**bruce nixon**

***2015 marks 800 years since the signing of Magna Carta.*** The year in which we celebrate the signing of Magna Carta provides an opportunity to create a great, new vision for British Democracy. We need to look forward as well as back. It is an opportunity for the British people to *"Dare to be great"* and create a democracy that will inspire the nation and make citizens believe again that it really is worth engaging and that voting counts.

Magna Carta is admired throughout the world as a symbol of liberty. It was the first occasion the people of England were granted rights against an absolute king. In 1791, Thomas Payne wrote his widely influential *Rights of Man*, which inspired reformers in Britain and elsewhere.

Yet, 224 years later, Britain is lagging behind; we are still oppressed by *"the powers that be"*. The past five years have demonstrated that the executive has too much power; people and Parliament have too little. Over half the population, 53% of whom are women, and black and ethnic minorities are under-represented. Despite the fact that girls are outstripping boys in exams, only one in five MPs are women. As we approach the centenary of votes for women, as Amanda Vickery says, there are more male MPs today than there have ever been female MPs (www.bbc.co.uk/guides/zy2987h).

In January 1917, a Royal Commission on Electoral Systems recommended proportional voting for the Commons back in 1910. A Speaker's Conference unanimously recommended a mix of AV and STV for elections to the House of Commons. Since then, numerous attempts to introduce fair voting have failed; Parliament is still unrepresentative and, as a

## the 21st century revolution

result, governments lack a mandate. It is 104 years since the 1911 House of Lords Reform Act, intended to be an interim measure, was enacted. We still have an unelected second chamber, with 850 members, compared with the House of Commons with 650.

***Until nations have a fully representative government, things are unlikely to change significantly for the better.*** A properly functioning democracy is vital to the health and wellbeing of a nation, particularly at a time when the world faces the biggest challenges in history and powerful vested interests are obstructive. The collective intelligence and creativity of human beings is enormous. But it is not fully engaged when we have a flawed system like this, and many people, especially younger ones, are turning their backs on voting.

***Radical change is in the wind.*** Almost certainly, the era of single party government is over. The future lies in collaboration. Similarly, the cosy relationship between Westminster and journalists may be over – the trend is towards social media. Despite the media largely ignoring the Green Party, yet obsessing with UKIP, a recent poll showed that 43% of Britons would consider voting Green. The British Election Study found that Green sympathisers are more likely to be female (57%), younger (average age 41, with 31% under 25), than supporters of other parties (www.britishelectionstudy.com). In the event, five million people voted Green and membership is increasing.

***A golden opportunity.*** This year's celebration of Magna Carta presents a golden opportunity. So are the elections and formation of new governments in many countries over the next couple of years. It is fitting that we celebrate this important moment in our history. But as I argued earlier, we need to look forward as well, not too much back. We have a very long way to go. I believe we need a comprehensive, written Constitution that includes all the major reforms and a new Bill of Rights. The Scots have shown us that people turn out and will vote if they believe it's worth it. Clearly, many Scots have no confidence in Westminster. Now is the moment to present comprehensive proposals for a democratic system that is obviously broken.

***A Citizen-led Constitutional Convention.*** The people of Scotland presented us with a great opportunity to get regionalisation and electoral reform back on the agenda. The Electoral Reform Society and Unlock Democracy are pushing for a Citizen-led Constitutional Convention, in which citizens are involved in proposing a new constitution.

***The State needs to make a new social contract with the British people,*** as it did after World War Two. The nation needs to inspire itself again. The Scots massively turned out to vote in their referendum. To restore public confidence in a broken system, comprehensive reform is required, not the cautious bit-by-bit approach adopted until now. We need a new written constitution, a new Magna Carta. Once again, we know what needs to be done. The solutions are the easy part; it's bold leadership that's needed to make it happen. This election year provides an ideal opportunity for citizens to demand that the parties commit to comprehensive radical reform.

***A written constitution and Bill of Rights.*** We need massive public campaigning to bring about radical change.

## the 21st century revolution

And we are not going to get it unless people are inspired to take action. For that, we need comprehensive reform that engages the imagination of a disillusioned nation. A succession of specific reforms is not acceptable. In an earlier chapter, I quoted Donnachadh McCarthy's calls for a 21st century Great Democratic Reform Act, barring politicians from becoming lobbyists for corporations claiming the Fourth Estate (the media) – this is already happening with the internet and social networking; academia freed from corporate interference and tax-havens closed.

**A new political party system is emerging.** The UK's political party system is at a time of considerable change. Parties are aware that they face a crisis as their membership shrinks, and they will have to change or die. Less than 1% of the UK electorate was a member of the Conservative, Labour or Liberal Democrat Party (House of Commons Library, 30th January 2015). Disenchantment with politics and politicians is dangerous. Failure to vote can lead to damaging extremism, racial bigotry and anti-immigration. In the UK, we have so much to be thankful for, especially our tolerance, and that we are one of the most successful multi-racial societies. There are also dangers arising from the most vulnerable not voting and, hence, not being represented in Parliament. Too often, party leaders are pandering to extreme elements and ill-informed back-benchers. Instead, they need to challenge them, especially on issues such as Climate Chaos, the ecological system, renewable energy, Europe and immigration.

**We need a very different kind of politics.** Structural reform will not be enough. We need a very different kind of politics compared with when party membership was at its peak after World War Two – 1951 Conservative 2.9m, Labour 876,000; 2011 Conservative 177,000, Labour 190,000, Lib Dem 66,000 (Source: Estimates based on party reports and House of Commons Library). Essentially, the mind-set of political leaders is patriarchal. They have a top-down mentality when they need to be hosts, as already argued. We need a new mind-set and different behaviour. In order to solve today's enormous problems, we need collaboration – not adversarial politics. To find solutions that work, diversity and difference needs to be valued. Parties, with their whips, by their nature, tend to suppress creativity. People have to toe the line.

Two women politicians in Spain foresee a different politics. Madrid's Manuela Carmena has promised a radical overhaul if she succeeds in becoming mayor of Madrid. Two of the most prominent voices leading democratic renewal in Spain belong to women. The new groups were born out of the "Indignado" ("Outraged") protests that swamped Spanish streets during recent years of economic crisis, campaigning against corruption and unemployment. At the time of writing, Manuela Carmena promises radical change if she succeeds in becoming mayor of Madrid. The time has come for *"a feminine way of doing politics"*, turning Madrid into an incubator of policies based on the values of coexistence, caring and non-aggression. *"To govern is to listen,"* says Carmena, repeating her oft-used phrase from the campaign. Ada Colau, whose Barcelona En Comú movement is likely to govern Barcelona said:

*"I think the world is increasingly realising the need to abandon vertical attitudes and move towards a deepening of democracy,"* and, *"Those are values of the new feminine*

### the 21st century revolution

*culture that will likely be the culture of the 22<sup>nd</sup> century."* (Thanks to Ashifa Kassam, Saturday 30<sup>th</sup> May 2015 – www.theguardian.com/world/2015/may/30/madrid-next-mayor-ex-communist-judge-manuela-carmena.)

**From opposition to consensus.** We need collaborative politics, not one-party domination. The time when one party forms a government and another party becomes the opposition should be over. All views need to be taken into account. MPs should represent the views of **all** their constituents, as Richard Wilson in Stroud, quoted earlier, said he would do if he won the May 7<sup>th</sup> election as a people-power MP. Online voting could be utilised by the electorate to tell their MP which way to vote on an issue. Every MP should do this or be ejected. Whips should be abolished. The Edinburgh City Government in 2012 provided an example. The leader of the Labour/SNP coalition made a contract *with* the capital to become a *"Co-operative Capital"*. That meant holding a two-way dialogue with residents about issues, encouraging petitions, establishing a Petitions Committee, creating a new culture of *"letting go"* and, wherever feasible, putting residents and service-users at the heart of service design and delivery (Electoral Reform Society, *Working Together – Lessons in how to share power*).

When I began this chapter, it seemed likely that the next government would be based on a confidence and supply agreement. A confidence and supply agreement is an agreement that a minor party or independent member of parliament will support the Government in motions of confidence and supply by voting in favour or abstaining (en.wikipedia.org/wiki/Confidence_and_supply). Possibly

#### bruce nixon

the end of one-party "majority" government has only been delayed. Our situation today urgently needs innovation and creativity. Creativity requires us to value diversity, inquiry, scrutiny, critical thinking and dialogue, not adversarial and often abusive debate. As argued earlier, finding ways forward that are most likely to work, to which everyone is committed, requires *"getting the whole system into the room"* (www.futuresearch.net). All stakeholders, all the expertise that is available, especially from people *"on the ground"* needs to be involved. That is a lesson that old-style political leaders find hard to learn.

Amongst the key reforms needed in the UK are:
1. Transformed political parties
2. Cleaned-up party funding
3. A fair voting system that reflects the diversity of all citizens
4. Equal numbers of women and men in Parliament and Government, roughly 50:50 and proportionality for Black and Ethnic Minorities (BEMs)
5. An elected and reformed Second Chamber to replace the unrepresentative, expensive, oversized House of Lords.

## *The Electoral Reform Society proposals*

The proposals of the Electoral Reform Society (ERS) respond to the need for political parties to transform themselves and clean up their funding. Significantly, the ERS report was built upon the thinking of its members, which it sought before producing its proposals – a model for how to create party policy. Here is a summary of their proposals:

***Open Up – The future of the political party.*** Party-political decline has been a subject of debate since the 1970s, based on evidence of falls in partisan identification and membership. But long-term trends are now combining with short-term triggers – party funding scandals, general political scandals, and the intensification of voter disengagement – to create the possibility that political parties are spiralling into terminal crisis.

The various ways in which parties should be responding to this threat can be boiled down to a simple message: they need to open up, even further and faster than they are already doing.

***Opening up organisationally.*** Parties need to continue to adapt to the new ways that citizens want to participate in politics. **Opening up party processes, letting go of top-down structures and embracing citizen-led activity** will help fundamentally shift the culture of our politics towards what citizens are demanding. An **increased reliance on supporters as well as members** is likely to be a part of this process. Changing party structures to allow supporters a more active and central role in campaigning is an important innovation.

Through new technology, parties have more opportunity than ever to connect with citizens directly, and on a more local basis. Social media enables parties to create a much-needed dialogue with citizens, and parties should do more to use these opportunities specifically to involve people in policy-making processes. Parties have greater opportunity to listen as well as talk, and should strive for genuine democratising of decision-making, avoiding the tendency to engage in consultation from above.

Parties also urgently need to **rebalance party funding in the interests of the many**, by diversifying their funding sources. They need to find a solution to keeping vested interests out so that ordinary supporters and members feel they too have a voice. Securing a wider funding base is likely to require consideration of a cap on donations and spending, and a fresh look at how public funding is allocated.

*Opening up electorally.* As well as expanding the wider public's role in their campaigns, parties should consider increasing outsiders' role in selecting candidates for election. Breaking the domination of small "selectorates" is an important part of opening up politics generally. Experiments with primaries and other ways of engaging non-members should be expanded.

Likewise, **changing the electoral system** would breathe new life into campaigning by moribund local parties in historically safe seats, and would give party supporters a reason to be politically active in areas where the voting system had previously made their votes worthless. It could also encourage a less negative campaigning style, which has greater potential to engage turned-off voters.

*Opening up legislatively.* While citizens want distinctive political parties, they also want a less combative, more open style of politics; one that is honest about the choices available and the reasons for decisions made. A change in the electoral system would see politics respond better to citizens' diverging political choices. It would be an acknowledgement that a multi-party system, which makes consensus and collaboration a necessary and normal part of politics, is what citizens want.

More open party politics could also include a greater role for citizens in decision-making. Parties should think about moving away from focus-group assessment of voter preferences, favoured by the centralising party organisations of the past, and consider instead the potential effects of engaging citizens directly in the decision-making process through deliberative, democratic mechanisms. This could help bring citizens closer to politics outside of election time.

***The new party model.*** The recent rise in membership numbers for those parties that are challenging the mainstream – UKIP, Scottish National Party (SNP), Plaid Cymru and the Green Party (the latter three led by women) – can teach us a lot about the future of political parties. Granted, a fair amount of these parties' appeal can be attributed to people's distaste for the mainstream parties or for Westminster politics in general. In some cases at least, these parties are more likely to experiment with opening up to their members and the wider electorate. As newer parties, they have fewer institutional barriers to opening up. And for some of them, it is in their very nature and constitution to be less hierarchical and more open. The emergence of these more modern challenger parties also reflects people's apparent preference for a multi-party system, where parties work together for the common good. Given these facts, and the picture presented by our members' and supporters' survey, we can begin to glimpse the outline of what the future holds for political parties. The mainstream, traditional parties are already moving towards this future. But if they are ever going to retain people's faith, they need to get there quicker.

**Cleaned up party funding.** Here is a summary of the proposals of the Electoral Reform Society (ERS). The public are sick to death of party funding scandals. It brings our democracy into disrepute, and we have to do something about it. An open, clean and fair model of funding the parties would give taxpayers far better value for money. It would ensure our politicians don't have to dance to the tune of trusts, union bosses or city interests. All the parties have been tainted. Scandal after scandal reveals an ever-growing arms race, where voters often appear to be come second to big donors. Left to themselves, the big parties have failed to find a solution. The ERS report (*Deal or No Deal: how to put an end to party funding scandals*) sets out the scale of public anger about the way parties finance themselves, and what the parties have to do to assuage that anger. Our polling from last year found that:

- 75% believe big donors have too much influence on our political parties
- 65% believe party donors can effectively buy knighthoods and other honours
- 61% believe the system of party funding is corrupt and should be changed

This level of dissatisfaction is clearly unsustainable, yet if something isn't done then the next party funding scandal is

## the 21st century revolution

just around the corner. Whatever the outcome in May, the next government has to get to grips with the way parties are funded.

Our report sets out what needs to be done. We propose three solutions, all of which have been recommended by previous committees looking into party funding, and have been shown by ERS polling and focus group research to command support from the public. These are:

- **A cap on the amount that anyone can donate to a party**, to end the big-donor culture that has led to scandal after scandal
- **An increased element of public funding for parties**, to bring the UK into line with other advanced democracies
- **A cap on the amount that parties are allowed to spend**, to end the arms race between parties at election time

There is huge public support for taking big money out of politics, so whichever party takes a lead on this could stand to benefit at the polls. The UK is way behind the rest of Europe on this, spending just a tenth of the European average on supporting parties and doing far less than most countries when it comes to limiting the influence of wealthy donors. It's time we caught up with the modern world and cleaned up party funding once and for all. (See more at: www.electoral-reform.org.uk/blog/deal-or-no-deal#sthash.U69NPJGF.dpuf)

***A fair voting system is the most urgent need***, if people are to have confidence in our political system. Parliament must represent the full diversity of the nation.

Clearly, it does not. The current front bench in the House of Commons is largely composed of people from privileged backgrounds, seen as out of touch. They have been successful in gaining power, but are not necessarily fit for the job. Privilege results in less able people in leadership. Greater talents may be lost; talent, evenly distributed in the human population, is wasted. The Electoral Reform Society believes that the Single Transferable Vote (STV) – The Alternative Vote (AV) system previously offered is too complicated and makes little difference – is the fairest method for determining the outcome of elections (www.electoral-reform.org.uk/?PageID=483). Another system widely used widely is Party List PR, which produces a more accurate reflection of votes. For that reason, I believe this system is preferable. Just before the 2015 General Election, pollsters, ORB, questioned over 2,000 people and found that 61% believe the system should be reformed so that smaller parties are better represented in Parliament. Another poll for the Electoral Reform Society by BMG Research showed that 74% of the public back the principle of votes proportionally translating into seats (www.electoral-reform.org.uk/press-release/three-quarters-want-more-proportional-voting-system-new-poll-shows).

Unlike the Suffragettes, who fought for the right to vote over one hundred years ago, going to prison if necessary, today we seem unwilling to fight for a fair voting system and demand it now!

***A Parliament that fully reflects the diversity of our nation.*** That means, as stated above, proportional representation. Part of this is up to the parties to bring about but some of it needs to be mandatory.

## the 21st century revolution

***50:50 Representation for women*** – all-women shortlists. Every constituency, enlarged to make this possible, would be required to return two MPs – one female, one male. Party leadership also needs to tackle this problem within their parties. To succeed, they also need to change the behaviour of politicians and the culture of Parliament. Proper representation at all levels is equally vital for Black and Ethnic Minorities (BEMs). For more information, see **Resources** at the end of this book.

A Speaker's conference was set up in 2008 to study the reasons why MPs were predominantly white, male and able-bodied. An interim report in July 2009 called for women to make up at least 50% of new candidates at the next General Election. The Labour Party has used all-women shortlists. But they proved controversial and all-women shortlists have continued to be criticised. In 1983, the Norwegian Labour Party mandated that *"at all elections and nominations, both sexes must be represented by at least 40%"*, and in 1994, the Swedish Social Democratic Workers' Party mandated *"every second name on the list a woman"*; male and female candidates would be alternated between each other on the party list of preferred candidates. In 1988, the Danish Social Democrats adopted representation of at least 40% for local and regional elections. If there were not sufficient candidates from each sex, the right would not fully come into effect; however, this party law was abolished in 1996 (Source: wikipedia.org/wiki/All-women_shortlists).

**Unaware sexism.** I believe these failures reflect the depth of unaware sexism. The time has come to start again. Every constituency, enlarged, should be required to return two MPs – one female, one male. Party leadership also needs to tackle this problem within their parties. The behaviour of politicians and the culture in Parliament also need to change. (For campaigns to bring about change, see Centre for Women in Democracy, Counting Women In 50:50 Parliament, and Operation Black Vote in the **Resources** section at the end of the book.)

***House of Lords reform.*** The following proposals are based on the Electoral Reform Society's proposals. The British governments have been trying to reform the House of Lords for over a century. In 2012, the House of Lords Reform Bill failed, but the issue is not going away.

The current House of Lords is grossly oversized and growing unstably as each incoming Prime Minister moves to restore party balance. It is too large to provide an effective and efficient second chamber. It currently has 765 active peers, dwarfing other second chambers around the globe. 525 peerages have been created since 1997, including 117 peerages since 2010. A change in government at the next election would see the number of peers in the Upper House increase dramatically again. Peers are members for life and are able to claim a tax-free attendance allowance of £300 per day, and travel expenses for the duration. Recent research has found that peers who did not vote at all in 2011 claimed a total of £46,685. In my view, the name "House of Lords" is inappropriate for a second chamber in the 21$^{st}$ century.

## *The purpose of a second chamber*

- An effective second chamber is part and parcel of an effective parliament and effective government.

## the 21st century revolution

Reform is a chance to preserve the chamber's vital scrutiny role and to actively enhance it with the legitimacy conferred by public election.
- The second chamber is intended to be primarily a revising and debating chamber with real but limited powers, making it an effective part of a constitutional system, rather than a source of authority in its own right. It is intended to be a more reflective, less tribal, political environment than the Commons, with a measure of independent judgement and seniority. Independence means that, while many members will generally follow their party whip, the ethos and rules of the House should tolerate judgement and dissent, and members should not be influenced by patronage (either in gratitude or expectation) or fear reprisals. Independence should also mean that the parties are not the only pathways into the second chamber.

### *Proposals*

- 100% elected. If you hold the power to pass laws, you should be chosen by the people who have to live by those laws.
- A reformed second chamber should represent the regions and nations of the UK, and that it should fairly represent the UK's diversity. No party should have an overall majority.
- At least 30% of the candidates presented in each region should be female.
- Elections using the Single Transferable Vote to ensure voters have a real choice between

candidates, small parties and independents, to improve representation and to avoid wasted votes.
- No reserved seats for Bishops of the Church of England, or indeed for any faith community leaders.
- Thresholds or other positive measures should be introduced to ensure diversity of candidates and to make sure the second chamber looks and feels more like Britain today.

We simply cannot have thousands of unelected politicians passing laws that the British people have to live by. The public are ready, with 79% supporting reform. Now it's our job to hold the politicians to account.

### *What is needed?*

- A 100% elected House of Lords.
- Elections using the Single Transferable Vote to ensure voters have a real choice between candidates, small parties and independents, to improve representation and to avoid wasted votes.
- No reserved seats for Bishops of the Church of England, or indeed for any faith community leaders.

Thresholds or other positive measures should be introduced to ensure diversity of candidates and to make sure the Lords looks and feels more like Britain today

**The role of the state** is to facilitate and enable citizens and communities to create a flourishing society. As I argue elsewhere, it is *not to consult* or use focus groups, the prevailing approach, *but to involve and engage* citizens. The effective way to enable change and solve problems is

## the 21st century revolution

to co-create solutions and *"get the whole system into the room"* in all its diversity, and find common ground and win; win ways forward (Future Search – www.futuresearch.net).

**New leadership.** Citizens should be enabled to make decisions about their communities, not developers, large retailers and supermarkets aided by remote boroughs or County Councils. Citizens should be in charge of how their towns are developed. The principle of subsidiarity applies – i.e. decisions are taken at the lowest level wherever possible.

*"The art of political leadership in the 21$^{st}$ century is to help grow the capacity of people to collectively make change happen, not impose change on them."* **Neal Lawson**, Chair of Compass

Political parties have a vital role but if they are to thrive and restore respect for themselves, they need to open themselves up to much more diverse membership and work much more like think and act tanks; encouraging free thinking, not limited by ideology and free from the influence of big donors. Their policies need to be developed democratically by involving their subscribers and members with the help of enlightened think tanks, not campaign advisers.

*"On social media, online and in communities, everyone now finds their voice. What these organisations know is that all of us together are smarter than any one of us and that experimentation is the quickest route to success. People are being the change they wish to see in the world."* **Neal Lawson**, Chair of Compass

**bruce nixon**

***A New Executive.*** Under the current system, a government is formed either by the party with a majority of MPs or a coalition is formed with a majority. In both cases, the Government does not represent the composition of Parliament or the wishes of all voters. Also, this arrangement results in complete changes when new administrations take over – they tend to wipe away the work of their predecessor, causing the frustration I described earlier in this book.

## Green Party proposals

The Green Party have put forward proposals that would mean all the parties working together. The Green Party want the central **Parliament itself to become the principal decision-making body of central government**. To do so, the central Parliament would elect committees, covering each of the major areas of government, and each committee would have its own convenor, elected by Parliament, who would take the place of the Secretary of State in the current system of government. The committee, assisted by a department staffed by civil servants responsible to the committee as a whole, would be responsible for day-to-day decisions in its area of responsibility. Major decisions, and new legislation, would need to be ratified by Parliament as a whole.

**A First Minister would also be elected by the central Parliament as a whole**, who would be responsible for chairing a committee, the Coordination Committee, of all the convenors of parliamentary committees. This body would be responsible for coordinating the work of the different committees, and for dealing with matters that affect them all, such as the allocation of public expenditure. **The First Minister would act as Head of Government**, in particular in dealings with other states. The central Parliament would also elect, as at present, an apolitical Speaker, who would act as Head of State (Source: policy.greenparty.org.uk/pa.html).

## *The Rights of Future Generations*

One of the greatest dangers in policy-making today is the failure to create long-term policies and protect the interests of future generations. This is particularly true of the threats of climate change and destruction of the ecosystem. Finland has created the following measures:

1. A newly elected government is required to state how they plan to address long-term problems.
2. A Committee for the Future whose role is to evaluate the long-term implications of current policies.
3. There is a public deliberative process in which the Government's statement is evaluated by the Committee, among other bodies, and Government ministers are required to give public justification of how their policies serve the interests of people living in the medium and long-term.

***The implications are profound.*** Measures such as these would make it much harder for a government to ignore the warnings of their own climate advisers and the UN climate scientists described in Chapters 2 and 3. Would any government risk creating new nuclear power plants or continue their use when there is no known way of safely disposing of their waste material?

Assertion of these rights particularly resonates with the quotation from a sixth-former in the Introduction. I believe that the rights should be foremost amongst the reforms proposed below.

(For the information above, I am indebted to Simon Caney's article, *Justice between generations: a research agenda*, published in *Inspires*, The Magazine of Oxford Politics and International Relations Alumni 2014. Simon Caney is Professor of Political Theory and Co-Director of Human Rights for Future Generations, Oxford Martin School, Oxford University – www.humanrights.ox.ac.uk. See also The Foundation for the Rights of Future Generations (FRFG) – www.intergenerationaljustice.org, and The Oxford Martin Programme on Human Rights for Future Generations – www.oxfordmartin.ox.ac.uk/research/programmes/human-rights.)

Here is a summary of the key reforms I believe parties should commit to:

---

### Key Constitutional Reforms in a written Constitution and Bill of Rights

- ***A Citizen-led Constitutional Convention***, as proposed by the Electoral Reform Society and Unlock Democracy, is an essential part of the process for constitutional reform.
- ***The Rights of Future Generations***, as described above, must be a part of a new Bill of Rights.

- **Proportional representation** for national, regional and local government. There are proportional voting systems in Germany, Denmark, Holland, Norway and Sweden. The Single Transferable Vote (STV), already used in Scotland and Northern Ireland, may be the best option. STV is designed to achieve proportional representation through ranked voting in multi-seat constituencies. Under STV, an elector has a single vote initially allocated to their most preferred candidate and, as the count proceeds and candidates are either elected or eliminated, the vote is transferred to other candidates according to the voter's stated preferences, in proportion to any surplus or discarded votes. The system provides approximate proportional representation, and minimises *"wasted"* votes by transferring votes to other candidates that would otherwise be wasted (Source: Wikipedia – en.wikipedia.org/wiki/Proportional_representation). As stated above, I prefer Party List PR, which produces a more accurate reflection of votes. It is argued that it is less democratic as parties choose who goes on the list. In my view, this is a decision to be made by a citizens convention.
- **50:50 Representation for women** – all-women shortlists. Every constituency, enlarged to make this possible, would be required to return two MPs – one female, one male. Party leadership also needs to tackle this problem within their parties. To succeed, they also need to change the behaviour of politicians and the culture of Parliament. Proper representation at all levels is equally vital for Black

and Ethnic Minorities (BEMs). For more information, see **Resources** at the end of this book.
- ***Parliament itself to become the principal decision-making body of central Government***, as described above. A First Minister would be elected by the central Parliament as a whole, who would be responsible for chairing a committee – the Coordination Committee – of all the convenors of parliamentary committees. This body would be responsible for coordinating the work of the different committees, and for dealing with matters that affect them all, such as the allocation of public expenditure. The First Minister would act as Head of Government, in particular in dealings with other states.
- ***Subsidiarity Power*** needs to be devolved to the people and communities through the principle of subsidiarity. The Oxford Dictionary defines it thus: *"A central authority should have a subsidiary, that is a supporting, rather than a subordinate function, performing only those tasks which cannot be performed effectively at a more immediate or local level."* IPPR believe in devolving power to local communities by the expansion of initiatives, like citizens' assemblies, that ensure the voice of ordinary citizens is heard in political decision-making. And directly elected mayors are the best means of holding local power accountable. (See Power Shift – www.ippr.org/juncture/power-shift-giving-people-the-power-to-reform-public-services)
- ***Devolution of power from Westminster.*** A thriving, balanced economy requires the devolution of power from Westminster. Further devolution of powers to

Scotland is inevitable. It needs to be increased in Wales and extended to the regions, not only to the North and West of England, but all city regions with City Mayors. It is already acknowledged that the great Northern cities need more autonomy and powers to raise money. Together, they account for more GDP than London. Greater Manchester is to become the first English region to get full control of its health spending.

- **An elected second chamber** replacing the unelected House of Lords explicitly formed as a reviewing chamber that can also initiate legislation. The criteria for nomination would be acknowledged expertise. The numbers of peers, now 850, should be considerably reduced.
- **A Senate of the Cities, Regions and Counties.** Ed Miliband proposed a Senate of the Cities, Regions and Counties and the break-up of the Treasury to devolve powers of taxing, spending and borrowing to them. The Senate could be sited in the Midlands. This presents an opportunity to get away from a beautiful and historic building that is hopelessly inappropriate for a modern, democratic institution and better used as a museum and library of democracy.
- **Referenda.** More frequent referenda, using digital technology on constituency and national issues, should be used, as in Switzerland.
- **Solving the EU's democratic deficit.** The Electoral Reform Society has put forward proposals for improving EU democracy. These include improving the representativeness of MEPs by using open-list voting systems, increasing the accountability of the

European Commission, and strengthening the role of EU citizens and national parliaments in decision-making. For full details, see *Close the Gap – Tackling the EU's democratic deficit* ([www.electoral-reform.org.uk/close-the-gap](www.electoral-reform.org.uk/close-the-gap)). Some of these proposals, suitably adapted, equally apply to UK's democratic deficit.

- ***An Oath of Service to constituents and the nation.*** MPs need to see themselves as servants of the people. On election, MPs should be sworn in and declare that they will, above all, serve the interests of the nation and represent the views of all their constituents. This can be facilitated by online voting and consultation.
- ***Digital Democracy.*** The UK Speaker's Commission has recommended online voting. **WebRoots Democracy** believes this would help boost voting and help overcome apathy, especially amongst younger people. They campaign for an accessible, informative, and interactive election website to help reach out to new voters.
- ***Interactive Democracy.*** In many countries, people are building bottom-up, inclusive democracy and voting systems. Amongst these is the DemocracyOS app, developed in Argentina and led by Pia Mancini; this is now being used in Brazil. It enables people to become informed, debate and then vote on the issues online. A similar platform called Pane is being used in Germany. Pia says we need to say *"No representation without conversation"*. (Thanks to *Hack the Vote* by Lee Williams in *The Independent*, 26th March 2015.) Registering to vote and voting made easier including doing both online.

- **Total Right of Recall**, giving constituents the right to recall MPs from Parliament who abuse their positions and power. The Coalition's proposals would give the final say to parliamentary committee rather than constituents. Grounds for recall would be limited to serious financial offences, or if an MP was sentenced to 12 months in jail. Voters should determine the reason for recalling an MP and have the final say. ERS say, *"We need to show Government that we won't stand for this watered-down version of recall. We will only accept a version that genuinely empowers people."*
- **War Powers.** Stronger powers are needed for Parliament to veto or approve the deployment of troops. In a democracy, decision-making should be open to scrutiny, accountable to elected representatives and, ultimately, to the people. The decision to send troops into armed conflict is one of the most serious any state can make. It could be made subject to a referendum. Parliamentary scrutiny is part of the constitutional principle of accountability, both to Parliament and the people, and ensuring that all issues are debated and scrutinised. Clearly not all information about the deployment of armed forces should be made public. Unlock Democracy proposed a new select committee, based on the model of the German Defence Committee. The Defence Committee in Germany is a departmental select committee, established in Basic Law, which, in addition to the scrutiny of bills and defence-related matters, has power to act as an investigative committee and consider any defence matter of its

choosing. The Defence Committee works in co-operation with the Foreign Affairs Committee, with access to relevant security information. (This is a short extract from Unlock Democracy's *"War Powers and Treaties Consultation"*. A longer version is to be found in Chapter 11: *Unlocking democracy* of my book, a *Better World is Possible* – www.brucenixon.com/betterworld.html).

- **Party funding**. There needs to be a cap on individual funding and complete disclosure – currently, loans do not have to be declared. Since party membership has declined from millions to mere thousands, parties depend on big donors for funding. Donations need to be capped and parties returned to individual members. Larger state funding could be acceptable.
- **The so-called "revolving door"**, including ministerial and Civil Service appointments, subverts democracy, corrupts politicians and has far too much influence on policy. There needs to be a statutory bar to these practices. Also, a statutory register of lobbyists is needed.
- **Votes from 16.** The right to vote should be extended to 16 and 17-year-olds, particularly if we want more young people to be engaged. Compared with older people, the young are more likely to vote for the Green Party or centre left policies.

## So what can we do?

**It is clear that we seven billion people need to take our power and act.** Do we choose to be victims or free spirits? We need to demand that governments do the right thing. It is in the nature of politicians to respond to public demand if there are votes in it. If the demands of citizens continue to be unheard, there is a risk of increasingly violent protest.

**ACTION:** Specifically, I suggest, support the proposals of the Electoral Reform Society. Lobby your MP, parliament representative, candidate or party. Sign up with influential organisations for news, reports and petitions: Compass, Democracy Now, IPPR, Local Works, Open Democracy, OurKingdom, and Unlock Democracy/Local Works. Further details are given in **Resources** at the end of this book.

# Chapter 10

# Conclusion – daring to be great

*"I've set myself a quest – to dare to be great. For me, that means being in service to something greater than the self. I believe we all have the capacity for greatness – and that to end the era of Ecocide requires the greatness of humans to stand up and say 'enough' to all that is causing mass damage and destruction in this world."* **Polly Higgins**

Does our affluent way of life in wealthy nations really justify all the harm and destruction it does to people and the planet, especially when it does not make us any happier? We know what makes us happy: simple things such as love, family, community, friendship, neighbours, meaningful work, nature, beauty, art in all its various forms, and the security in which to bring up a family. These are the things most human beings crave for. Yet the current economic system does not allow most people in the world enough time for them or sufficient means. Nor does it lead to security.

**A new narrative.** Once, we believed the world was flat; once, we believed our Earth was the centre of the Universe. These beliefs are long gone. Today, the narrative is about GDP, austerity, tactical politics, competition and

## the 21st century revolution

power. It is about dominating nature through so-called science, competing with and exploiting other nations, imposing Western democracy with bombs, threats and counter-threats, weapons of mass destruction to make us feel secure, adversarial politics, winning elections, one party dominating, then another. The daily news is full of depressing stories, disease and starvation, poverty and greed, having more, a bigger car, a bigger house, and having the latest gadget.

Instead, we need to live lightly on our planet. We are all one; we are part of nature, humble stewards whilst we are here, not masters of it. Nature is a perfect self – regulating system. If we abuse it, rather than work with it, we court disaster.

The world is yearning for a new narrative. We need a vision of a better world. More and more people want to build consensus, to have dialogue about the way forward. They want consensus politics, not divisive, adversarial politics. They want to resolve conflict without violence.

Frequently, I notice such new narrative is being spearheaded by women. Younger people in particular are abandoning established ways of doing things, forming new progressive movements, and creating new ways of doing business, sometimes co-operatives. The internet, for all its failings, is where progressive discourse is taking place and creative proposals and innovations are emerging.

*"There is an Indian proverb or axiom that says that everyone is a house with four rooms; a physical, a mental, an emotional, and a spiritual. Most of us tend to live in one room most of*

*the time but, unless we go into every room every day, even if only to keep it aired, we are not a complete person."* **Rumer Godden**, author of *A House with Four Rooms*

In his article, *Unconditional Empathy* in Resurgence & Ecologist, March/April 2015, **Satish Kumar** talks of love and idealism, and love of planet Earth.

*"The whole Earth is my friend, and the whole world is my friend. ... Friendship is the only glue to hold humanity together. Through the philosophy of friendship, we deeply realise that we are all connected, we are all related, we are all interdependent. The entire planet Earth is our home, and we are members of this one Earth community and one human family. You might call me an idealist. Yes, I am an idealist. What have realists achieved? Wars? Poverty? Climate change? The realists have ruled the world for too long and have failed to achieve peace and prosperity for all. So let us give idealists a chance and let friendship be the organising principle of our world."*

Satish said we need idealists; realists have not achieved much.

All of us need to dare to be great. There are many people throughout the world who are daring to be great. But too few, if we are to overcome the vested interests that resist the positive change. All of us can take responsibility and get engaged in our own unique way – through initiatives, modifying our way of life and activism. When others see it, it becomes infectious.

## the 21st century revolution

One thing we must have no doubt about is that, if we are to avoid environmental catastrophe, world leaders must agree on urgent and concrete actions at the United Nations Climate Change Conference, COP21, to be held in Paris, 30th November to 11th December 2015. The most important decision they must take is to agree, through a binding commitment, that two degrees is the upper acceptable limit of global warming on Earth. All other decisions taken in Paris will follow as a consequence of that agreement. However, world leaders have consistently failed us. This year, there must be a breakthrough at last. They need our active support. We all have a part to play.

**What can I do?** I am often asked this question. Here are some questions that may help you decide. First, find yourself a place where you can quietly reflect.

**What is my vision?** What kind of world do I want in my lifetime and for future generations?

**What is my purpose in life?** Why am I here?

**What matters most to me?** What am I most passionate about?

**How can I make the biggest difference?** Have a look at the links given in some chapters and the **Resources** at the end of this book. What skills and assets do I bring? Where can I make a difference or exert an influence? With whom would I like to build a supportive partnership? Change-makers need to give each other loving support.

#### bruce nixon

***How will I feel when I take effective action to help bring this about?***

***Finally, given what I love doing and have to offer, what shall I do?***

Bruce Nixon October 2015

# *Resources*

**Action on Sugar** is a group of specialists concerned with sugar and its effects on health. It is successfully working to reach a consensus with the food industry and Government over the harmful effects of a high-sugar diet, and bring about a reduction in the amount of sugar in processed foods. Action on Sugar is supported by 23 expert advisers (www.actiononsugar.org) We also need **Action on Salt** and **Health**: excessive consumption of salt causes 1.65 early deaths annually (www.actiononsalt.org.uk)

**AltGen** supports 18-29-year-olds to set up workers' co-operatives as a way of reclaiming control over our work and creating a more equal and sustainable economy.

We are told time and time again that we are the generation without a future – the first ever to inherit an economic reality worse than the generation before. The good news is that every crisis creates opportunities and we've got ideas to help turn this situation around!

Let's stop competing and start co-operating. Let's come together and start creating an alternative future: one where we are in control of our working lives, get paid to do what we love, and have a positive social impact (www.altgen.org.uk).

**Better Transport** is highly successful in promoting affordable, sustainable transport. It aims to reduce the environmental and social impact of transport by encouraging less use of cars and more use of public transport, walking and cycling. It promotes integrated transport to help people get to work more quickly without driving (www.bettertransport.org.uk).

**Campaign for Dignity in Dying.** We campaign to change the law to allow the choice of an assisted death for terminally ill, mentally-competent adults, within upfront safeguards. You can help us make that change happen (www.dignityindying.org.uk).

**Campaign to Protect Rural England** campaigns for a beautiful, living countryside. We work to protect, promote and enhance our towns and countryside to make them better places to live, work and enjoy, and to ensure the countryside is protected for now and future generations (www.cpre.org.uk).

**Centre for Alternative Technology** works for a Zero Carbon Britain. CAT is an education and visitor centre, demonstrating practical solutions for sustainability. They cover all aspects of green living: environmental building, eco-sanitation, woodland management, renewable energy, energy efficiency and organic growing (www.cat.org.uk).

**Centre for Women in Democracy** believes that women are under-represented at all levels of public life and public decision-making and works to change this. We:
- commission, carry out and publish research and reports on women in public life, both in the UK and around the world

## the 21st century revolution

- run workshops to inform women about, and encourage them to become involved in, public decision-making
- prepare and submit evidence and other papers to consultations and inquiries carried out by Parliament, Government, political parties and other bodies
- work with partner organisations to promote our objectives. (www.cfwd.org.uk)

**Citizens Income Trust** proposes radical reform of the welfare system, suggesting the annual spend on benefits should be distributed equally among all citizens, regardless of their income or employment status. Under their proposals, 0-24-year-olds would receive £56.25 per week; 25-64-year-olds would receive £71 per week; and those 65 and over would receive £142.70 per week. Analysing figures from the 2012-13 financial year, the cost of such a scheme is projected at around £276bn per year – just £1bn more than the annual welfare budget that year –making the implementation of a citizen's income close to revenue and cost neutral (citizensincome.org).

**Compass** is for those who want to build and be a part of a Good Society – one where equality, sustainability and democracy are not mere aspirations, but a living reality. We are founded on the belief that no single issue or political party can usher in this future alone as the world is too complex to change with one solution or one organisation. Compass is a place where people come together to create the visions, alliances and actions that will build our Good Society (www.compassonline.org.uk).

**bruce nixon**

**Compassion in World Farming** was founded over 40 years ago in 1967 by a British farmer who became horrified by the development of modern, intensive factory farming.

Today, we campaign **peacefully** to end all factory farming practices. We believe that the biggest cause of cruelty on the planet deserves a focused, specialised approach – so we only work on farm animal welfare (www.ciwf.org.uk/about-us).

**Counting Women In** campaign is aiming for 50:50 gender representation at all levels of national, local and devolved government. We will be fighting to ensure women have an equal presence and voice in British politics (www.countingwomenin.org/index.php/counting-women-in). Also support

**50:50 Parliament** (www.5050parliament.co.uk) and **Women 50:50** in Scotland (www.women5050.org), and sign their petitions.

**Crowdfunder** is an alternative means of funding, allowing individuals to take their ideas forward and make them a reality with the power of the crowd. Crowdfunder enables people with a great idea to raise the money they need in return for "rewards". The public can back an idea with pledges of money and project owners can "thank" their backers with rewards that reflect the money contributed. The reward can be a product, service or experience that is produced by the project. Whether you are a community group, business, social enterprise, school, charity, or are just an individual with a fantastic idea then we can help you

## the 21st century revolution

raise the funds needed for your project (www.crowdfunder.co.uk).

**DemocracyOS.** Pia Mancini is one of the founders of the Net Party, a political party headquartered in Argentina. She is also a co-founder of DemocracyOS, which are free source decisions in order to give more weight to the opinions of citizens (direct democracy). Her political goal is to make a *"democracy of the 21$^{st}$ century"* that would result in greater impact of citizens in politics, notably through new technologies, with the internet as the main element (democracyos.org). **WebRoots Democracy** is an independent, non-partisan organisation, campaigning for the introduction of online voting in Local and General Elections. We are an organisation that intends to reverse growing political apathy and low electoral turnout in the UK, particularly amongst young people. Whilst political apathy has a variety of causes, we recognise that we live in an age of distraction and rapid, technological advances. As such, we are also campaigning for an accessible, informative, and interactive election website to help reach out to new voters. We intend to highlight and research the causes of political apathy amongst young people and boost their voter turnout to ensure that they have a strong electoral voice in the UK (webrootsdemocracy.org).

**Democracy Now** provides our audience with access to people and perspectives rarely heard in the US corporate-sponsored media, including independent and international journalists, ordinary people from around the world who are directly affected by US foreign policy, grassroots leaders and peace activists, artists, academics and independent analysts (www.democracynow.org/about).

**Electoral Reform Society** and **Unlock Democracy** work closely together. **The Electoral Reform Society** operates on a simple premise – that politics can be better than it is. We are campaigning for a better democracy. Our vision is a representative democracy, fit for the 21$^{st}$ century. We know that every year that passes with our steam age political system still in place is a missed opportunity for the people of Britain (www.electoral-reform.org.uk) **Unlock Democracy** campaigns for continuing constitutional reform, strengthening the power of local communities, and a modern and fair democracy. Through their successful campaign for the Sustainable Communities Act, the power of local democracy and local communities will be strengthened (www.unlockdemocracy.org.uk and **Local Works** – www.localworks.org).

**Eradicating Ecocide.** Ecocide is the extensive destruction of ecosystems to such an extent that peaceful enjoyment by inhabitants of a territory is severely diminished. Polly Higgins campaigns to make ecocide the fifth crime against peace. The proposed Ecocide Law will create a new framework within which business and the global economy can operate in harmony with the Earth's ecosystems, using them as renewable resources that will last forever, rather than commodities to be exploited just once. Her two books are possibly the most important for the 21$^{st}$ century (eradicatingecocide.com and pollyhiggins.com).

**Ethical Consumer.** Their thorough research gives you the lowdown on corporations and enables you to campaign. That forces them to change (www.ethicalconsumer.org).

## the 21st century revolution

**Fair Tax Campaign.** Fair Tax is at the heart of society. Around £12 billion is lost to the public purse each year via corporate tax avoidance. Fair Tax is campaigning for all parties to commit to a Tax Dodging Bill. The Fair Tax Mark is about UK business leading the world in setting a new standard in responsible tax practice – from the smallest shop to the biggest multinational. It's the label for good taxpayers. It is for companies and organisations that are proud to pay their fair share of tax. Wherever you see the Fair Tax Mark, you can be sure that a company is open and transparent about its tax affairs and seeks to pay the right amount of corporation tax at the right time in the right place. Fair Tax Mark aims to offer businesses that know they are good taxpayers (or want to work towards becoming one) the opportunity to proudly display this to their customers (www.fairtaxmark.net).

**Garden Organic**, formerly known as Henry Doubleday Research Association – a valuable resource and campaigning for organic gardeners and others interested in healthy, organic and local food, as well as flowers especially grown in their own gardens (www.gardenorganic.org.uk).

**Global Justice Now**, a respected, influential NGO and reliable source of information, and for campaigning on global issues, particularly poverty and economic injustice. Formerly **World Development Movement** (www.wdm.org.uk).

**Global Power Shift.** Global Power Shift is the starting point for a new phase in the international climate movement. First, hundreds of climate leaders from around the world gathered in Istanbul to share stories, learn skills, and sharpen strategies. These leaders have now returned to their home countries to spark a wave of convergences, campaigns, and mobilisations for climate action (globalpowershift.org and www.worldometers.info/world-population).

**GM Freeze campaign**, supported by an alliance of 120 national organisations who share the public's deep concern over the speed at which genetic engineering is being introduced into food and farming (www.gmfreeze.org).

**Green Alliance.** Green Alliance is an environmental think tank, working to ensure UK political leaders deliver ambitious solutions to global environmental issues. This is a home for debate on UK environmental policy and politics. As well as providing our own view, we invite leading commentators from business, government, NGOs and academia to share their thoughts and ideas. The views of external contributors are not necessarily those of Green Alliance (green-alliance.org.uk).

**Harrison Owen's** Open Space Technology is an invaluable process, enabling large groups to work productively together. (His classic books: www.openspaceworld.org Also Spirit and Peace: www.practiceofpeace.com)

**Help for Heroes.** Our mission is to deliver an enduring national network of support for our wounded and their families. We will inspire and enable those who have made sacrifices on our behalf to achieve their full potential. The war in Afghanistan may be over, but for those who have suffered life-changing injuries, their battles are just beginning. We've estimated that, of the 220,560 individuals deployed to Afghanistan and Iraq between 2001 and 2014, up to 75,000 servicemen and women (and their families) may need our support in the future. We will not let them fight these battles alone (www.helpforheroes.org.uk, and in the USA, www.help4heroes.org).

**Homes for Britain Campaign** brings together those who believe everyone has a right to a decent, affordable home to call their own. Our support comes from people across the country and we've joined forces with organisations from every corner of the housing world. For decades, we have failed to build enough new homes. We are currently building half the number needed every year. Many of us can't start a family because we can't afford to move. Many adults still live with parents, our first home still a distant dream. Many of us live in overcrowded homes, struggle to afford to keep a roof over our heads, or even become homeless. The housing crisis is affecting people from all walks of life and all parts of the country (homesforbritain.org.uk).

**Human Rights Watch** defends the rights of people worldwide. We scrupulously investigate abuses, expose the facts widely, and pressure those with power to respect rights and secure justice. Human Rights Watch is an independent, international organisation that works as part of a vibrant movement to uphold human dignity and advance the cause of human rights for all (www.hrw.org/about).

**Institute for Public Policy Research (IPPR)** is a UK progressive think tank. The purpose of our work is to assist all those who want to create a society where every citizen lives a decent and fulfilled life. It involves addressing unjustified inequalities, constructing an economy that serves society, challenging concentrations of power, maintaining a vibrant national and local democracy open to the world (www.ippr.org).

**James Robertson,** *"grandfather of green economics".* Perhaps the best single resource on radical, economic reform, including money, sustainable taxation, debt, banking and citizens income (www.JamesRobertson.com/news.htm – also www.globaljusticemovement.net, and for Islamic perspective, free of interest and relevance to sustainability, www.islamic-finance.com).

**Jubilee Debt Campaign** is part of a global movement, demanding freedom from the slavery of unjust debts and a new financial system that puts people first. Our vision Inspired by the ancient concept of "jubilee", we campaign for a world where debt is no longer used as a form of power by which the rich exploit the poor. Freedom from debt slavery is a necessary step towards a world in which our common resources are used to realise equality, justice and human dignity (jubileedebt.org.uk).

**Kings Fund.** The King's Fund is an independent charity working to improve health and healthcare in England. We help to shape policy and practice through research and analysis; develop individuals, teams and organisations; promote understanding of the health and social care system; and bring people together to learn, share knowledge and debate. Our vision is that the best possible care is available to all (www.kingsfund.org.uk and www.kingsfund.org.uk/about-us).

**Land Value Taxation Campaign**, a non-party organisation. Land value tax has a significant contribution to make to sustainable taxation and could fund a citizens' income. This campaign promotes the adoption of land value taxation in the UK and understanding of its economic benefits. The campaign is concerned with informing and influencing politicians, academics, journalists and other opinion-formers. (www.landvaluetax.org/the-campaign; Land Value Scape (www.landvaluescape.org) is a further source of information.)

**Landworkers' Alliance** (landworkersalliance.org.uk) is a producer-led organisation of small-scale producers and family farmers who use sustainable methods to produce food, fuel and fibre. We raise awareness of the role that our members play in providing food security, environmental stewardship, livelihoods, strong communities, animal welfare and high-quality, affordable food. We work to overcome the obstacles facing land-based workers by campaigning for better policy for agro-ecology and food sovereignty. We campaign for the rights of small producers and a better food system. We are members of **La Via Campesina**, the international peasant farmers union, and work in solidarity with our fellow land workers across the globe (www.eurovia.org/?lang=en and www.eurovia.org/?lang=en).

**Liberty**, was founded in 1934 and we are a cross party, non-party membership organisation at the heart of the movement for fundamental rights and freedoms in the UK. We promote the values of individual human dignity, equal treatment and fairness as the foundations of a democratic society. Liberty campaigns to protect basic rights and freedoms through the courts, in Parliament, and in the wider community. We do this through a combination of public campaigning, test case litigation, parliamentary work, policy analysis and the provision of free advice and information (www.liberty-human-rights.org.uk).

**Margaret Wheatley** offers the lessons from nature, change, leadership, resistance, courage, diversity, life balance and global issues, articles, books, events and simple processes to facilitate learning and taking effective action (www.margaretwheatley.com and www.berkana.org).

**Marvin Weisbord, Sandra Janoff and Future Search** – their classic books on large group processes are amongst the most valuable I have read (www.futuresearch.net).

**Mothers at Home** is a not-for-profit campaigning group run by volunteers. We hope our campaign gives support and encouragement to anyone involved in family care and/or who believe strongly in family life. We are funded entirely by membership donations and we ask you to consider joining us, as we are now in danger of not being able to continue for much beyond 2015, despite having campaigned for well over 20 years. Our campaign is needed now more than ever before, with more and more families struggling to have the resources they need (time, decent pay levels, affordable housing, fair family taxation and allowances) to raise their children in the face of anti-family policies from central Government (www.mothersathomematter.co.uk).

**New Economics Foundation (NEF).** My top choice; it is an inspiring independent think-and-do-tank that researches and demonstrates real economic wellbeing. It

## the 21st century revolution

aims to improve quality of life by promoting innovative solutions that challenge mainstream thinking on economic, environment and social issues. It puts people and the planet first. It succeeds by working in coalitions and influences politicians of all parties, Government and the media (www.neweconomics.org).

**Open Democracy.** In Britain, it is often asserted that we have a free press. This is not completely true. There are numerous subjects that national newspapers and broadcasters either ignore or devote token attention. It is a digital commons, not a magazine – a public service on the web, not a commodity. It is an independent, public interest, not-for-profit; a counter to the corporate media, champions human rights, seeks out and debates forms of democratic change, delights in good ideas vigorously debated and argument backed by investigation, critiques vested interests, supports pluralist inclusion without populism and tries to a give voice to those marginalised, tries neither to blink at the crisis of government nor cultivate alarmism, opposes fundamentalisms, including market fundamentalism, regards the freedom and liberty of others as our own, practices "openness", rather than grasp at stultifying "neutrality", publishes under Creative Commons licensing, supports peace-making and reconciliation, is committed to global education and encouraging good and creative writing, welcomes a range of forms to enable us to respond swiftly and interrogate deeply (www.opendemocracy.net).

**Operation Black Vote** exists to ensure we have greater racial justice and equality throughout the UK. We work specifically, but not exclusively within the democratic and civic framework to deliver our objectives. We seek to inspire BME communities to engage with our public institutions in order to address the persistent race inequalities we face in areas such as: education, health and employment. Our work spans a number of areas including voter registration, lobbying politicians, mentoring schemes and political leadership programmes. After 15 years of campaigning, we are viewed as a beacon of hope and support for our own communities (www.obv.org.uk/about-us).

**Oxford Real Farming** (orfc.org.uk), **The Campaign for Real Farming** (www.campaignforrealfarming.org). *"Real Farming"* is shorthand for *"Enlightened Agriculture"*, defined as: *"Farming that is expressly designed to provide everyone everywhere with food of the highest quality, forever, without wrecking the rest of the world."* The aim is to help to create *"convivial societies within a flourishing biosphere"*. The methods of Real Farming are those of Agro-ecology, in which individual farms are conceived as ecosystems, and agriculture as a whole is seen as a key component of the biosphere.

**Penal Reform.** New Economics Foundation (NEF) and Centre for Justice Innovation are leading an ongoing investigation, *Beyond Crime and Punishment*. (To read this and get involved, go to www.neweconomics.org/projects/entry/better-courts and www.neweconomics.org.)

**People's Assembly** is a broad, united, national campaign against austerity, cuts and privatisation in our workplaces, community and welfare services, based on general agreement with the signatories. It is linked to no political party, committed to open non-sectarian working and

## the 21st century revolution

dedicated to supplementing, rather than supplanting, trade union, student, pensioner and community opposition to austerity measures (www.thepeoplesassembly.org.uk).

**Population Matters.** We promote a voluntary and gradual reduction in global human population to a level that enables an acceptable quality of life for all, protects wildlife and is ecologically sustainable (populationmatters.org/about/pm-goals).

**Positive Money** is a movement to democratise money and banking so that it works for society and not against it. Our current financial system has left us with the highest personal debt in history, unaffordable housing, worsening inequality, high unemployment and banks that are subsidised and underwritten with taxpayers' money. We believe that these problems have a common root: money (www.positivemoney.org and *Sovereign Money – paving the way for a sustainable recovery*).

**Positive News** (positivenews.org.uk). Quarterly newspaper devoted to positive international news. Combine this with **Resurgence & Ecologist** magazine and you won't be a pessimist and you will be well-informed (www.resurgence.org/magazine/resurgence-ecologist.html).

**Resolution Foundation.** The goal of the Resolution Foundation is to improve living standards for the 15 million people in Britain on low and middle incomes. To achieve this, we conduct rigorous research, analysis and policy development to inform public debates and influence key decision-makers in government, the private sector, and civil society (www.resolutionfoundation.org).

**Rethinking Economics** is an international network of students, thinkers and citizens, coming together to demystify, diversify, and invigorate economics. We aim to demystify and diversify economics in the public eye; to educate ourselves and other students in a more reflective economics; to inspire divergent economists to engage with one another in debate; and to promote a politics of responsibility within academic economics (www.rethinkeconomics.org).

**RoadPeace** champions the rights of road crash victims, and works to increase public awareness and campaigns for real road safety to reduce the causes of road crashes (www.roadpeace.org).

**Robert Greenleaf Servant Leadership Centre** promotes servant-leadership (www.greenleaf.org and in UK, www.servantleadership.org.uk).

**SAVE Britain's Heritage.** SAVE has been campaigning for historic buildings since its formation in 1975 by a group of architects, journalists and planners. SAVE is a strong, independent voice in conservation, free to respond rapidly to emergencies and to speak out loud for the historic environment (www.savebritainsheritage.org).

**SAVEGREEKWATER.** In Greece, there is a campaign to prevent the privatisation of water (www.savegreekwater.org/?page_id=29). They argue that international experience has shown that the privatisation of water has resulted often in the skyrocketing of prices and in some cases in the deterioration of water quality. Although the trend in Europe is the return of water supply companies' management to the hands of municipalities, once again, with a 20-year delay, the Greek state is being "modernised" towards policies of the past.

**Share Action** is a ground-breaking charity that promotes Responsible Investment by pension funds and fund managers. Bringing together leading charities, trade unions, faith groups and individual investors, our aim is to catalyse a shift at each level of the investment chain, so that Responsible Investment becomes the norm. Share Action has a strong track record of persuading major investors to increase shareholder activism on environmental, social and governance issues. Today, Share Action is recognised in the UK as the leading NGO that monitors and engages with the investment industry (shareaction.org).

**Shelter** helps millions of people every year who are struggling with bad housing or homelessness – and we campaign to prevent it in the first place. We're here so no one has to fight bad housing or homelessness on their own (http://england.shelter.org.uk).

**Soil Association** is the UK's leading membership charity, campaigning for healthy, humane and sustainable food, farming and land use (www.soilassociation.org and **Save Our Seeds**). EU rules and major corporations are reducing the number of seed varieties available for us all to grow, damaging biodiversity and driving small seed suppliers out of business. Sign up to help us fight them before it's too late (www.soilassociation.org/saveourseeds).

**Sustrans** is UK charity working on practical projects to help reduce motor traffic, a national Cycle Network and Safe Routes to School (www.sustrans.org.uk).

**Transparency International.** Our mission is to stop corruption and promote transparency, accountability and integrity at all levels and across all sectors of society. Our core values are: transparency, accountability, integrity, solidarity, courage, justice and democracy. Our vision is a world in which government, politics, business, civil society and the daily lives of people are free of corruption (www.transparency.org).

**Transition Town Network** is a leading exemplar of people all over the world, taking their power to bring about change. It is a resource and inspiration for communities wanting to start grass roots initiatives for responding to the challenges of Peak Oil, peak everything, ecological destruction and Climate Chaos. It provides a focal point for towns, villages, cities and localities around the world as they implement their own Transition Initiatives. There are now 1,400 official Transition town groups in 40 countries but many more unofficial groups (www.transitionnetwork.org). One of these is **Transition Town Berkhamsted**, where I live, which started in early 2007 and flourishes (www.transitionberkhamsted.org.uk).

**Vandana Shiva**, an internationally-renowned campaigner, upholding the rights of small farmers, especially women, against unscrupulous transnational corporations, teaches farmers how to prosper through organic methods. Navdanya, the research foundation she inspired, offers international courses (www.navdanya.org).

## the 21st century revolution

**War on Want** fights poverty in developing countries in partnership with people affected by globalisation. We campaign for human rights and against the root causes of global poverty, inequality and injustice. Poverty is political. The decisions of politicians in rich countries can mean life or death for people in developing countries. We have the power to reshape the global landscape – to ensure that people across the world can live in justice and peace (www.waronwant.org).

**Women for Refugee Women** challenges the injustices experienced by women who seek asylum in the UK. We work to empower women who have sought sanctuary in the UK to speak out about their own experiences to the media, to policy makers and at public events. We aim to give a voice to women who are all too often unheard and unseen (refugeewomen.com).

**World Future Council** is an ethical voice for the needs of future life, and to pass on a healthy planet and just societies to our children and grandchildren (www.worldfuturecouncil.org).

**World Watch** is a leading source of information on environmental, social, and economic issues, and how to achieve an environmentally sustainable and socially just society (www.worldwatch.org).

More resources are provided in my book, *A Better World is Possible*, at www.brucenixon.com/betterworld.html, where there are articles by me and other writers.

## *Appendix 1 – Systems Thinking*

Central to this book is my view that systems thinking is essential if we are to address the challenges we face and grasp the opportunities. It is a process of understanding how systems influence one another within a whole. In nature, systems thinking examples include ecosystems in which various elements, such as air, water, movement, plants, and animals, work together to survive or perish. In organisations, systems consist of people, structures, and processes that work together to make an organisation healthy or unhealthy.

Systems thinking is an approach to problem-solving, by viewing problems as parts of an overall system, rather than reacting to a specific part, outcomes or events, and potentially contributing to further development of unintended consequences. Systems thinking is based on the belief that the component parts of a system can best be understood in the context of relationships with each other and with other systems, rather than in isolation.

In systems science, it is argued that the only way to fully understand why a problem or element occurs and persists is to understand the parts in relation to the whole. It views systems in a holistic manner that requires an understanding of a system by examining the linkages and interactions between the elements that compose the entirety of the system.

### the 21st century revolution

This summary is based on *Systems Thinking* at en.wikipedia.org/wiki/Systems_thinking. Peter Senge's book, *The Fifth Discipline*, describes how it can be applied in organisations.